Religion & Life

Sarah K. Tyler
Gordon Reid

With thanks to the governors, headmaster, staff and pupils of Alleyn's School, Dulwich.

Philip Allan Updates
Market Place
Deddington
Oxfordshire
OX15 0SE

Tel: 01869 338652
Fax: 01869 337590
e-mail: sales@philipallan.co.uk
www.philipallan.co.uk

Design by Neil Fozzard

Printed by Scotprint, Haddington

Environmental information
The paper on which this title is printed is sourced from managed, sustainable forests.

P00432

Contents

Introduction

This book gives you the information you need to do well in your Edexcel Religious Studies GCSE exam on religion and life. The material in it is relevant for:

- Unit A: Religion and life based on a study of Christianity and at least one other religion — in this case, Islam
- Unit B: Christianity
- Unit C: Catholic Christianity

It covers the four compulsory topic areas on which you have to answer questions in the exam, as well as the two options which you can do in the exam or as coursework:

- believing in God
- matters of life and death
- marriage and the family
- social harmony
- religion and the media (can be examined or covered by coursework)
- religion, wealth and poverty (can be examined or covered by coursework)

These correspond exactly with what you will find in the specification and appear in the same order. 'Religion as expressed in art, music or literature' is not covered in this book as this topic can only be done as coursework.

The exam

In your exam you will have to answer either four or five questions, depending on whether you are offering coursework. Each of the first four questions is worth 20 marks and is broken down into four parts, worth 2, 6, 8 and 4 marks respectively:

- The 2-mark question usually asks for a definition of a key term or idea.
- The 6-mark question asks you to show your knowledge of a belief or issue.
- The 8-mark question aims to see how well you understand the issues and beliefs.
- The 4-mark question asks you to consider a point of view and weigh up arguments for and against it, giving your own opinion in a carefully considered way.

If you are not doing coursework, you will have to answer a fifth question in the exam, which requires longer answers. The question is broken down into three parts, worth 4, 8 and 8 marks:

- The 4-mark question is knowledge based; it asks you for information and facts about the topic.
- The first 8-mark question asks you to show your understanding of the topic.
- The second 8-mark question is evaluative, again suggesting a point of view and asking you to analyse it and make a balanced judgement.

You need to work quickly in the exam as there is a lot to cover. If you offer the fifth specification area in the exam, instead of doing coursework, remember that you are being tested for quality of writing as well as content.

Coursework

If you opt for the coursework option, you will be answering a similar set of questions to those you will find in the exam, but you will need to write more and go into more depth. The specification suggests 1,500 words for a piece of coursework, although you can, of course, write more than that. The coursework questions are broken down into two parts, again worth 20 marks overall.

- Part (a) consists of three sub-questions that are knowledge and understanding based and worth 12 marks.
- Part (b) consists of one 8-mark evaluation question, as in the exam.

You are likely to get plenty of guidance from your teacher about coursework. Don't rush it at the last minute; take time to perfect it and include some information that no one else in your class has in theirs. There is a lot of coursework out there and you need to make sure that yours stands out.

Using this book

There are six sections in this book, each of which follows the same basic format. The main part of each section provides you with the information you need to answer questions on the topic, including definitions of key words. Most sections include quotations from religious texts and other sources, and you should aim to learn a few of these for each specification area.

Each section covers a range of views on the topic. This is important: to get top marks you must show that you are aware of and can discuss differences in belief on even some of the most central issues in religion, regardless of whether you yourself agree or disagree.

At the end of each section there is a range of questions and activities:
- **Sample questions and answers** The questions included here represent the type of questions you will have to answer in the exam. The answers given are generally longer than you are likely to write in the exam, but they show you the best type of answer you could give.
- **Further questions** These provide more examples of the type of question you will have to answer in the exam. You should use them for exam practice.
- **Class activities** These are intended to be tackled in class under your teacher's guidance. Your teacher will supply you with any materials you need to complete these activities and organise you into pairs or groups as appropriate.
- **Homework** These tasks are intended to be carried out at home. Some require access to the internet.

At the end of this book there is a glossary and a list of useful websites:
- **Glossary** This contains all the key words and definitions found through-out the book. Use this for reference and as a revision aid.
- **Useful websites** These are sites which you may find it helpful to refer to during your course. Some are very specific; others are more general.

Believing in God

Religion is about belief and how people choose to live their lives. It may be defined as a belief in a God (or gods), which leads believers to live their lives in a certain way. The way believers live is supposed to reflect the teaching of their religious **faith**. However, the existence of God cannot be proved (**verified**) in the way we can prove other things, by scientific testing or by using our senses (**empirical evidence**). True belief or faith is based on trust — people knowing God in their own way through what they have experienced, thought, read or been told.

Christianity and Islam are both monotheistic faiths — this means Christians and Muslims believe there is one God. Muslims also believe that Muhammad was the 'Seal of the Prophets' — the last prophet of God to whom was given the complete and final revelation of the Qur'an. Anyone who converts to Islam must say the words of the Shahadah — 'La ilaha ilallah wa Muhammadur rasul al-Lah' ('There is no

Key words

Empirical evidence
Evidence confirmed using the senses

Faith
Belief in something (e.g. God) without proof

Verified
Proved to be true

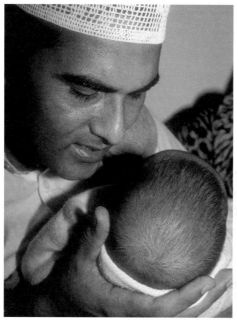

The first words a Muslim baby hears are those of the Shahadah

God but Allah, and Muhammad is the Prophet of God') — and these are the first words a Muslim baby hears. The life of a Muslim should be dedicated to the love and service of Allah.

That which you have been given is but a fleeting comfort of this life. Better and more enduring is that which Allah has for those who believe and put their trust in Him; who avoid gross sins and indecencies and, when angered, are willing to forgive; who obey their Lord, (and) attend to their prayers.

(Surah 42:36–39)

Christian faith is distinguished by the belief that Jesus is the Son of God and that God can also be known through the person of the Holy Spirit. This does not mean that God is divided into three gods. Rather, Jesus and the Holy Spirit are the ways in which the one God can be known to believers, in three distinct persons. This belief is known as the Trinity.

Christianity is the largest world religion, followed by approximately a third of the world's population. Islam is increasing in popularity, and not just in traditionally Muslim countries. After the terrorist attacks of 11 September 2001, the number of Muslim converts in the USA increased considerably, and there are 400,000 Muslims in the state of Texas alone. At present, approximately 21% of the world's population is Muslim.

Coming to believe in God

For many religious believers, God is the Supreme Being and the creator of the universe. People who believe in the existence of God are likely to have come to that belief through one of the following ways.

A religious upbringing

Children brought up by religious parents may well believe in God from their earliest years. Many religious believers adopt the faith and beliefs that their family and community hold. For many believers, family life is bound together by that faith, which is an important part of family tradition, handed down from one generation to the next.

For Christians, one of the main purposes of **marriage** is to have children and to bring them up in a secure and loving Christian environment, so that they will come to believe in God. The Bible is clear on the importance of family relationships: 'Honour your father and your mother' (Exodus 20:12). Similarly, the Christian Churches teach about the importance of the family for religious belief: 'The family is the community in which, from childhood, one can learn moral values, begin to honour God and make good use of freedom' (Catechism of the Catholic Church).

Key word

Marriage
The legal union of a man and a woman

Family members often share their beliefs with members of the wider religious community. This helps to preserve belief in God and maintain the importance of religion for future generations. It also unites the family and the community and gives them a shared identity.

Families and communities may share lifestyle and practices too. Religious communities may pray and worship together, and celebrate religious festivals and sacraments. In times of need, they take care of each other.

An adult receiving baptism

In some denominations of the Christian Church, families introduce their children to their faith through baptism. This is an initiation ceremony that makes someone a member of the Christian community. In the baptism service, either water is poured on the believer's head or the believer is immersed in water. This symbolises the washing away of their sins and a new start in life. People may be baptised as infants or much later in life. Some denominations do not carry out infant baptism and baptise only adult believers, often in a

Key word

Prayer
Communicating
with God
through words
or meditation,
alone or with
others

baptistery (a special pool built for this purpose). This is because they believe that every individual must make their own decision to believe; it cannot be made on their behalf. At an infant baptism, Christian parents promise to bring up their children in a Christian environment and to teach them the main truths of their faith. When adults are baptised, the congregation encourages them, perhaps by reading specially chosen Bible passages or saying a personal **prayer**.

In Christian communities children are encouraged to believe in God through going to Sunday school and church, while adults receive encouragement from Bible study groups and other shared activities. They also join their fellow Christians to celebrate the great religious festivals such as Christmas and Easter.

As a child, a Muslim is taught that everything should be done for Allah and not to gain credit or praise from others. The model for Muslims is the life of Muhammad, and they should try to live according to that which is Al-Sunnah — what Muhammad himself did or taught. It is the responsibility of Muslims to learn as much as possible about their faith, following the example of experienced Muslims and asking questions at home, at school and in the mosque. Muslims should seek to tell others about Islam and be able to explain the significance of everything they do.

Central to all Muslims are the five pillars of Islam. The first is the Shahadah (the statement of belief in Allah and Muhammad, his Prophet). The other four are Salah (saying the compulsory congregational prayers), Zakah (a specific charity paid yearly for the benefit of poor Muslims), Hajj (pilgrimage to the holy city of Makkah), and Sawm (observing the fast during the month of Ramadan).

Religious experience and miracles

Many religious believers claim that God reveals himself to human beings in a number of different ways. People may experience God when they read the message of sacred writings, during worship or through special experiences. Throughout the centuries people have claimed that they have encountered God through dreams and visions, heard his voice within them, seen **miracles** or had life-changing **religious experiences**.

Religious believers claim that God reveals himself or makes himself known through revelations. These may be general revelations that are available to everyone through their conscience or experience of the world around them, or they could be special revelations given by God to a certain individual or group, such as visions. Religious experiences vary from one person to the next, but many are life changing.

Charismatic worship may involve very personal religious experience

Today, many people grow up without a religious family or community, yet still find faith in God through personal experience. They believe in God because they feel that, somehow, they have experienced him in a special way that has utterly convinced them of his existence. Recent research suggests that about a quarter of all adults believe they have experienced God in some way in their lives, whether through answered prayers or by simply feeling that God was with them.

There are many varieties of religious experience. Some people claim to have had a **mystical experience**, such as hearing God's voice, or seeing a vision of a religious figure, such as Jesus. This type of experience gives people the feeling that that they have been contacted by God in a special way.

> Woe is me! For I am lost; for I am a man of unclean lips, and I dwell in the midst of a people of unclean lips; for my eyes have seen the King, the Lord of hosts.
>
> (Isaiah 6:5)

Some people come to God after having a **near-death experience**, where they have died for a short time and believe they have been to the afterlife before being resuscitated, usually during a surgical operation. Many have reported meeting a religious figure, usually, but not always, within their culture's religious tradition and, as a result, have become believers.

Key words

Miracle
An event that violates natural law and has a beneficial outcome

Mystical experience
Hearing God's voice or seeing a vision of a religious figure

Near-death experience
An experience during clinical death when a patient may see bright lights, a religious figure and sense being sent back to earth

Religious experience
An experience that conveys a sense of the presence of God

Key words

Charismatic experience
An experience inspired by the Holy Spirit, including speaking in tongues and prophecy

Conversion experience
Transferring faith from one religion to another, or from non-belief to belief in God

Numinous experience
An experience that conveys a sense of awe and wonder

Alternatively, a person could have had a **charismatic experience**. This is when people feel God working within them through the power of the Holy Spirit. It is sometimes shown through phenomena such as speaking in tongues (worshipping God with the Holy Spirit leading them), prophecy (giving a message from God about the future) or healing people through the power of God.

Others claim to have had a **conversion experience**, in which they are converted from one faith to another or from no faith at all into a belief in God. Such people have the feeling that there is something inside them turning their lives towards God. Conversion experiences can be dramatic, such as that of the apostle Paul, who was temporarily blinded by God. He changed his name from Saul to Paul after his experience.

> As he neared Damascus on his journey, suddenly a light from heaven flashed around him. He fell to the ground and heard a voice say to him, 'Saul, Saul, why do you persecute me?'
> 'Who are you, Lord?' Saul asked.
> 'I am Jesus, whom you are persecuting,' he replied.
>
> (Acts 9:4–5)

Other people, however, feel the presence of God after years of quietly searching for him rather than during a sudden transformation. Such a religious experience is often described as **numinous** — the person has feelings of awe (holy fear and wonder) and a sense of either being very close to God or an awareness of just how far away they are from him. This often leads to an increased love for God and a desire to serve him. John Wesley, the founder of the Methodist Church, had such an experience:

> About a quarter before nine, while he was describing the change which God works in the heart through faith in Christ, I felt my heart strangely warmed. I felt I did trust in Christ, Christ alone, for salvation; and an assurance was given me, that he had taken away my sins, even mine, and saved me from the law of sin and death.

Many people claim to have experienced a miracle in their lives, where God appears to have acted, usually in response to prayer. Miracles are said to be actions carried out by God that break natural law. Natural law is something

St Paul's conversion was dramatic

that happens so frequently within the world, like rain falling, that it would be considered to be a miracle (beyond the workings of nature) if it happened differently or failed to happen. For religious believers, God is the reason why miracles happen. If someone is healed of a serious illness and there is no medical explanation, it may be convincing enough to lead someone to believe in God.

Jesus performed miracles as part of his teaching, to help people to understand who he was and what he was saying. In the Bible he is seen curing the sick, calming storms, feeding crowds with very little food and raising the dead.

Believe the miracles, that you might know that the Father is in me, and I in the Father.

(John 10:38)

You might like to read about some of these miracles in the Bible:
- Mark 4:35–41 (the calming of the storm)
- Luke 8:40–56 (Jairus's daughter and the woman with the haemorrhage)
- Matthew 14:13–21 (the feeding of the 5,000)
- John 11:1–44 (the raising of Lazarus)
- Acts 3:3–10 (the healing of the crippled man)

Many religious believers claim God performs miracles. Charismatic preachers, such as Benny Hinn, hold huge rallies where hundreds of people claim to have been healed. However, many critics say that they are not miracles at all but hoaxes.

Benny Hinn

Benny Hinn is a world-renowned evangelist (a preacher of the Christian message) who, as well as conducting vast 'miracle crusades', has a daily programme on a US television network called *This Is Your Day*. He is also the author of many bestselling books, including *Good Morning, Holy Spirit*. He is a controversial figure, and many well-known and respected Christian writers and preachers speak out strongly against him and his claims while others are very supportive of him.

Benny Hinn was born in Israel to a Greek father and Armenian mother and raised in the Greek Orthodox faith. However, when the family moved to Canada, he was 'born again' and so, he claims, eventually were his parents. He received visions of himself preaching before huge crowds, and he has continued to claim many experiences where God has spoken to him directly and has made clear the special role that God has for him. Hinn's critics have apparently identified many inconsistencies in the information he has given about his early life. They have strongly criticised his teaching which, they say, is often based on false understandings of the Bible, although Hinn has claimed special 'revelation knowledge' — that is, God making something new known to him.

Hinn was strongly influenced by miracle workers of the 1960s and 1970s, especially by Kathryn Kuhlmann, who carried out miracle crusades and attracted thousands of followers. He was particularly impressed by the technique she adopted of encouraging people to fall down, apparently under the power of the Holy Spirit. This is called being 'slain in

the Spirit' and looks dramatic when it happens on stage. Hinn blows on willing volunteers or pushes them over with the exclamation, 'Substance!', knocking them down again when Hinn's helpers get them to their feet. Critics claim this has nothing to do with the power of God, but is a hypnotic technique used to persuade people to fall by the power of suggestion. Critics also feel that some of Hinn's own staff fall simply as part of his act. It creates an atmosphere of excitement and expectation among the crowds, who then believe that anything is possible — including disabled people getting out of their wheelchairs. One source claims:

> An elderly Hinn follower was initially turned away from one entrance to the ARGO stadium in Sacramento, California, because she had not given enough money to enter there. Later, on the stage, she was slain in the Spirit and while she was lying on the floor a huge man, likewise slain, landed on top of her, breaking her leg. In 1993 in Basel, Switzerland, Hinn prophesied over a man with cancer that he had many years to live. He died 2 years later. In Nairobi…four patients released from a hospital to attend Hinn's Miracle Crusade died while waiting for prayer.

It is not only apparently false claims to miracles that have drawn much negative attention towards Hinn. He preaches a doctrine often known as 'prosperity teaching', which claims that God wants to bless everyone with financial prosperity — usually as a result of giving amply to Hinn's crusades. An investigative documentary, *Miracles*, broadcast on Channel 4 in 2001 (see page 102) shows

Hinn telling the crowd that economic disasters will take place, but those who have given faithfully to God's work will be spared their effects. He then invites people to place donations in the buckets that the stewards pass around, reminding them that if they are giving by credit card not to forget to include 'the expiration date'.

Hinn's lifestyle is said to be lavish, although he justifies flying in his private plane on the grounds that he would 'wear out very quickly' if he travelled commercially. Hinn also writes in his autobiography, *He Touched Me*, that, at a time when his own ministry faced bankruptcy, he heard God telling him to give generously to other ministries and charities. He did this, even though members of his board resigned because of his decision, but as a result, he believes, God blessed his own work and their debts were paid within months.

Muslims believe in miracles too and one of the greatest was the giving of the Qur'an in its perfect form. Muhammad is also said to have performed miracles and these include splitting the moon, giving miraculous supplies of food and water, providing lights to guide his companions on a dark night, and appealing for rain in a time of drought.

Miracles are claimed within Islam today. These are very different from those in modern Christian traditions. In 1997, a Huddersfield teenager sliced open a tomato, the inner veins of which apparently spelt out in Arabic 'There is only one God' and 'Muhammad is the messenger' on each side. Similar messages are reported to have appeared in melons, aubergines, honeycomb and eggs. In one account, a young man in the Netherlands bought 5 kilos of beans and found the word 'Allah' written on several of them. He donated them to a mosque, where they were used to make a meal for the community. The imam later reported, 'We could serve as much as we wished, and the supply was still not exhausted.'

Religious believers claim that a loving and all-powerful God would perform miracles in order to meet the needs of those who believe in him. God is said to be **immutable** (unchanging) and **eternal**, so, if he performed miracles in biblical times, there is reason to believe he continues to perform miracles today.

Key words

Eternal
The belief that God exists without beginning and end

Immutable
The belief that God's nature and characteristics do not change

Prayer

Prayer is the way in which religious believers communicate with God. It may involve words or silence. Believers feel closer to God through prayer, especially when they listen to God as well as speak to him. Christians see themselves as part of God's family and it is, therefore, important for them to have a relationship with God. Prayer is an essential part of Christian belief and worship.

Christians meet together to pray and study the Bible

Christians believe God is a loving father who wishes to help his children. Equally, Christians love God and want to share their lives, hopes and anxieties with him. Jesus himself prayed, and encouraged his followers to do the same. The most famous Christian prayer, the Lord's Prayer, was taught by Jesus to his followers. For Christians, praying enables them to talk to God and to draw strength, guidance and support from him. It helps them to express their love for him.

There are many different types of prayer. The main ones are:
- adoration and worship — praising God
- thanksgiving — giving thanks for all that God has given
- intercession — asking God to meet the needs of people
- petition — praying for your own needs and asking for God's help
- confession and penitence — asking for forgiveness for the wrongs you have done and promising not to do them again

Prayers may be private and individual, or they may be corporate, when a number of people pray together. They may be formal or spontaneous, when people make up a prayer to meet a particular need.

Some believers practise meditation. This is a quiet form of prayer, where believers focus their thoughts entirely on God. The person meditating simply sits still and concentrates on God.

Christians believe that although God is a loving father who listens to and answers prayers, this does not mean every prayer will be answered, just like a good parent does not give in to every request from a child. Christians believe that God answers prayer in his own way and that he always does what is best. Jesus said the following about prayer:

> Ask and it will be given to you; seek and you will find; knock and the door will be opened to you. For everyone who asks receives; he who seeks finds; and to him who knocks the door will be opened.
>
> (Matthew 7:7–8)

A Muslim at prayer

Muslims are called to pray five times a day, having made special washing preparations beforehand known as wudu. Many schools and workplaces provide prayer rooms where Muslims can pray during the day. In a mosque, Muslims kneel on prayer mats as a sign of respect and, wherever they are, they pray facing in the direction of the Ka'bah in Makkah.

In most cases, people pray because they already believe in God's existence but, on some occasions, people may come to believe in God because someone else has told them about a prayer that was answered. Alternatively, people may just try for themselves to see if a prayer might meet a need. If they believe God has heard and answered their prayer, they may feel they have good reason to believe in God themselves.

The appearance of the world

When some people look at the world, the solar system and nature, they get the feeling that these things have somehow been caused or designed deliberately by some great intelligence, a cosmic designer whom they call God.

Such people believe that God created the universe and life for a purpose and that they are not here just by chance. There must be a reason for humans to be here; life must have a purpose: 'For since the creation of the world God's invisible qualities — his eternal power and divine nature — have been clearly seen, being understood from what has been made' (Romans 1:20).

Religious believers use the fact that the world exists to support their belief in God. Their argument is:

- nothing happens by itself — everything needs a cause
- the universe must need a cause
- only God could be powerful enough to cause the universe to come into existence
- therefore, God exists

This is the argument from **causation**. It is often called the Cosmological Argument. Its success is based on the truth of the claim that everything is caused by something else. The start of everything is God.

> In the cosmos as we experience it, it is obvious to us that some things change. Now, whatever changes must be changed by another. And if that other itself changes, then that too must be changed by another. But this cannot go on to infinity. You eventually have to arrive at something that is unchanging. This is God.
>
> (Thomas Aquinas, *Summa Theologica*)

It is not only the existence of the universe that leads some people to believe in God. The features of the universe, say many believers, seem to show they have been designed. In other words, they have a purpose of some kind — functions that someone designed and made them for. This means all the parts of the universe have been put together in exactly the right way, so that they work perfectly.

The argument from **design**, which is also called the Teleological Argument, runs like this:

- design requires intelligence and thought
- the universe appears to have been designed
- therefore, a being with intelligence and thought must have designed the universe
- only God could design something as complex as the universe
- therefore, God exists

The great scientist, Isaac Newton, looked at his own thumbprint. He knew that the design of the pattern on his thumb was unique and that no two people are the same. This convinced Newton that there was a designer of the world.

The philosopher, William Paley, compared the universe to a watch. He claimed that just as a watch must be designed, so must the world, because it has so many complex and special features. This view encourages people to look closely at the universe and to decide whether it is more or less likely to have come about by chance than to have been created by God.

The search for the meaning and purpose of life

A belief in God comes to some people after a long search for the meaning and purpose of life.

At some point in their lives, many believers have asked themselves questions like 'What is the purpose of life?', 'Why do we suffer and die?' and 'What is of real value in life?' For some, the answers to these questions lie in the existence of God and the feeling that, without God, life seems meaningless. This is known as faith — believers have to trust in God rather than in themselves and the world — and because God cannot be seen or touched, this is a difficult test of religious faith. Both Christians and Muslims stress the importance of the need for faith. Faith is tested in many ways. For Muslims, being able to deal with these tests without losing faith is essential.

The presence of religion in the world

Others have argued that the very fact that there are so many people who believe in God is, in itself, a good reason to accept that he exists. Although the various world religions offer different ways of coming into a relationship with God, most share many common truths. It could be argued that the probability of God's existence increases the more people there are who believe in him.

While it may be the case that religious belief can be the cause of war and strife, it also leads to communities of people who share a common belief and moral code and who are prepared to make sacrifices in the name of God — such as changing their career and lifestyle to help others in God's name. This in itself may be seen as convincing evidence for God's existence; people are prepared, at considerable personal cost to themselves, to change the way they live for the sake of God.

Reasons not to believe in God

Many people choose not to believe in God and a variety of arguments suggest that God did not create the universe.

Theists, atheists and agnostics

Key words

Agnostic
Someone who is unsure whether there is sufficient evidence to prove the existence of God

Atheist
Someone who does not believe that God exists or that there is a convincing case for the existence of God

Theist
Someone who believes in the traditional idea of God, usually as omnipotent, omniscient and benevolent

Many believers claim that God created the universe and that he is the cause of everything. A religious believer is sometimes called a **theist**. Theists argue that the universe did not come about by accident. Nature is so complex and intricate that it must have been designed by a supreme being — God.

An **atheist** is someone who does not believe in the existence of God. Atheists argue that science explains the universe much better than religion. For them, the universe was not designed — it has evolved.

An **agnostic** is someone who believes that it is impossible to know for certain whether or not God exists. As there is no reliable evidence one way or the other, for an agnostic the only position to maintain is that of not knowing.

In Islam, the position is different. Denial of Allah (At Ta'teel) could include denying his perfection or attributes (for example, any of his 99 names), failing or refusing to worship him, or worshipping other gods or human beings alongside him. Regarding anything as being equal to Allah is called shirk and is forbidden in Islam. Claiming that the world can be explained without reference to Allah would also constitute At Ta'teel. Debates about the existence or otherwise of Allah are not tolerated within Islam, as they are considered blasphemous:

> Whoever possesses the [following] three qualities will have the sweetness of faith: (1) The one to whom Allah and His Apostle becomes dearer than anything else; (2) Who loves a person and he loves him only for Allah's sake; (3) Who hates to revert to atheism [disbelief] as he hates to be thrown into the fire.

Non-religious explanations of the world

The most famous non-religious explanation of life on earth is the theory of natural selection, which is commonly associated with the scientist Charles Darwin. He argued that all living things descended from common ancestors and that each generation has evolved from more primitive forms of life. Some religious believers reject this theory because it seems to do away with the need for God. It suggests that living things were not fully formed when they were created, but evolved gradually from chemical matter with no action from God.

A modern-day supporter of Darwin's theory is Richard Dawkins. He is particularly well known for his attacks on religious interpretations of the world and human life, which he considers to be based on myths and therefore completely unreliable in providing an explanation. Furthermore, he suggests that if people are happy with religious explanations, they are actually closing off their minds to the possibility of finding other, more exciting, suggestions in the field of science. Dawkins believes that science holds the answers to all questions of existence, and if it does not appear to do so, we should study science more deeply.

Modern science also supports the theory of the Big Bang as an explanation for the universe. The Big Bang was an explosion of matter that took place some 15 billion years ago, and from which the universe has been expanding and evolving gradually.

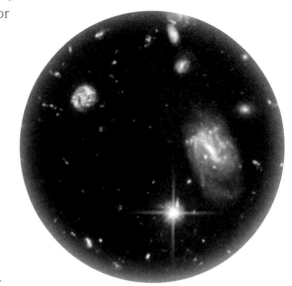

However, it is possible to argue that the Big Bang and natural selection were the means God used to bring about the universe. This is called compatibilism — making scientific and religious explanations compatible with each other.

Do miracles really happen?

Religious believers argue that miracles offer real proof for the existence of God. However, atheists argue that science makes it difficult to believe what the Bible says and that miracles can be explained in other ways. If someone recovers unexpectedly from an illness, the religious follower may claim that this is because God has performed a miracle, but it might equally be explained medically. Similarly, some people may regard a lucky event or a coincidence as God intervening in their lives. But why would a loving God do miracles for some people and not for others?

Prayers that go unanswered

If people's prayers go unanswered, it may make them feel that perhaps God does not exist after all. An atheist may say that if a loving God exists, he should answer the prayers of all those who truly believe. People pray for healing, peace and an end to suffering, yet illness, war and suffering still happen. Unanswered prayers are a real test of faith for believers, who may be forced to come up with a reasonable explanation of why God may have answered their prayers with a 'no' rather than a 'yes'.

The problem of evil and suffering

Evil is the most extreme form of badness and suffering. It causes pain, grief or damage. There is much good in the world, yet every day on the news we see instances of great evil and suffering: wars, **poverty**, terrorism, starvation, crime, disease and much more. Throughout human history, there has always been evil and suffering, from the plagues to the Holocaust, slavery to world war. Evil and suffering can also be on a smaller, personal scale, with people experiencing pain and suffering at different times in their lives.

There are two main types of evil:

- **natural evil**: suffering caused by nature and beyond human control, for example famine, disease, earthquakes and volcanoes
- **moral evil**: evil actions performed deliberately by humans, causing suffering to others, for example murder, rape, war and theft

Sometimes, these two types of evil overlap, for example, when war (a moral evil) causes famine due to poor harvests (a natural evil), or when cancer is caused by manmade pollution. It is worth considering whether death is an evil or an essential part of the natural order of things. What would be the alternative if we never died? Would it be desirable or not? What about animal suffering? Why are many of us concerned when we hear about cruelty to animals?

Of course, not all suffering is caused by evil. For example, people may suffer out of personal choice, by running into the road without looking, or by taking harmful drugs. In a similar way, people may suffer because they live in difficult circumstances, such as being born in a poverty-stricken country or with a physical handicap.

The existence of evil and suffering in the world is one of the strongest arguments against the existence of God. This is because

Key words

Moral evil
Evil acts performed by humans

Natural evil
Events in the natural world that cause suffering

Poverty
Lack of money, land and possessions

The events of 11 September 2001 shocked the world

God is said to be all-powerful and all-loving. If this is true, then perhaps he should prevent evil and suffering. Since there is evil and suffering, perhaps God does not exist after all?

Benevolent
All-loving

Omnipotent
All-powerful

Omniscient
All-knowing

The problem can be expressed as follows:
- God is thought to be all-loving (**benevolent**), all-knowing (**omniscient**) and all-powerful (**omnipotent**).
- If God is benevolent, he would want to remove evil and suffering.
- If God is omniscient, he would know how to remove evil and suffering.
- If God is omnipotent, he would be able to remove evil and suffering.
- Therefore, both God and evil cannot exist.
- However, evil and suffering do exist.
- Therefore, God cannot exist.

This is a very strong argument as it challenges the existence and characteristics of God. If God exists but is not all-powerful and all-loving, why should people worship him? This is such a difficult question that religious believers have tried to seek a convincing explanation for why God allows evil to continue and yet is still all-loving and all-powerful.

Christian responses to evil and suffering

Christians believe God gave humans free will. This means that people can choose what they do and decide whether to do good or evil. Humans can, therefore, choose to love, help, encourage and create, or they can choose to hate, fight and destroy. Above all, they can choose whether to believe in God and serve him.

In the Bible, Genesis 1–3 explains this idea clearly. It suggests that God created the world and human beings perfectly and that he gave humans free will. The first humans, Adam and Eve, used their free will to disobey God. When they did so, evil and suffering were brought into the world by their freely chosen actions and, as a result, they were separated from God: 'So the Lord God banished [Adam] from the garden of Eden to work the ground from which he had been taken' (Genesis 3:23).

The Bible suggests that the source of evil and suffering is Satan. God does not destroy evil because that would take away the free choice he has given to everyone. Instead, Christians believe God has provided humans with a way to make things right. Jesus died so that humanity could be freed from sin and evil and could come back into a full relationship with God. His innocent suffering and death ended the power that evil and suffering had over humanity.

> For God so loved the world that he gave his one and only Son, that whoever believes in him shall not perish but have eternal life.
>
> (John 3:16)

Some Christians believe that life in this world is a sort of test to prepare them for eternal lifewith God. Christians believe the choices they make have an influence on what happens to them throughout their lives. They can grow closer to God or further away from him. The existence of evil and suffering enables people to develop good qualities, such as helping the poor, comforting the dying, feeding the hungry, taking care of the environment, and taking a stand against people who come to represent evil.

Many Christians find it difficult to understand God's reasons for allowing evil and suffering to continue in a world that he controls. However, if, as the Bible says, God is truly a God of love, then even if his reasons are not clear to humans he works with a final plan in view, which is all-good and all-loving.

> He will wipe every tear from their eyes. There will be no more death or mourning or crying or pain, for the old order of things has passed away.
>
> (Revelation 21:4)

Muslim responses to evil and suffering

Islam also teaches that evil is linked with free will. Satan was an angel with free will who rebelled against Allah and was thrown out of **heaven**. He now uses evil to tempt human beings away from Allah. Humans are constantly tested to see how they

Key word

Heaven
A place where, after death, humans can live eternally in the presence of God; other interpretations suggest that heaven is an *idea* in the minds of believers rather than an actual place

respond to evil and suffering. In the twentieth century, the Islamic philosopher Muhammad Iqbal suggested that goodness would not be possible without evil. The evil in the world is meant to be overcome, but we should not ask why there is evil, because without evil there could be no moral or spiritual development.

Asian tsunami, 26 December 2004

Few people will ever forget the terrible events of Boxing Day 2004, when a massive tsunami (an ocean earthquake that measured about 9 on the Richter scale) devastated a vast region of south-east Asia. The images of this natural disaster, which wiped out whole communities, were like those we are more used to seeing in the cinema. But this event was not conjured up by the imaginations of Hollywood producers, it was real and it was affecting millions of people.

Not surprisingly, the event drew a wide response from religious believers, thinkers and leaders across the world. It was a graphic example of natural evil and, as

the Archbishop of Canterbury, Dr Rowan Williams, suggested, how could it not test people's faith?

In the *Daily Mail* on 28 December 2004, Terry Waite wrote: 'Today, many will be asking the age-old question, "Why?" Why do the innocent suffer; why does God permit suffering; what is the point of this endless sequence of blood, sweat and tears across the generations?' Waite's answer was to turn to the book of Job in the Old Testament/Jewish Bible which tells the story of an upright and honest landowner who suffered every possible misfortune that could be thrown at him. Despite his suffering, however, Job maintained his faith in God. Waite observes how suffering comes to everyone in some degree: 'We don't have to look for suffering, it will find us, and the sad fact is that some people, through no fault of their own, will indeed suffer more than others.' The answer, he suggests, is not to blame God, but to recognise that suffering is 'part and parcel of this world and human life and will remain so until the end of all things'.

Waite argues that for Christians the answer to suffering lies in the incarnation — the fact that God became human in the person of Jesus and entered the world of innocent suffering. He admits that this does not make suffering more understandable, but argues that it does show how faith can give hope and

transformation in times of suffering. God does not forsake people who are suffering, just as he did not forsake Jesus.

Jonathan Sacks, the chief Rabbi, addressed the issue in *The Times* on 1 January 2005. He also used the book of Job which led him to the observation that the question humans need to ask in the face of such a disaster is not 'Why did this happen? but 'What then shall we do?' Sacks suggests that although a disaster of this type brings grief and suffering, it also gives humans the chance to 'help the afflicted, comfort the bereaved, send healing to the injured, and aid those who have lost their livelihoods and homes. We cannot understand God, but we can strive to imitate his love and care.'

Questions and activities

Sample questions and answers

1 What does the term 'miracle' mean? (2 marks)

A miracle is an act of God that breaks the laws of science and nature, has a good outcome and is said to help people to believe in and have faith in God.

2 Outline the main beliefs of atheists. (6 marks)

An atheist is someone who does not believe in the existence of God. Someone might be an atheist because they believe that, with all the evil and suffering in the world, there cannot be a loving God. For example, if there was an all-loving and all-powerful God, he would want evil and suffering to end. However, because evil and suffering exist, perhaps there is no God. Someone might also be an atheist because they feel that modern science 'proves' that the Bible isn't true and that there is no God. Alternatively, a person might be an atheist because in the past they prayed to God at a time of crisis but their prayers were not answered. This might have led them to think there is no God.

3

Explain why a religious experience may make someone
believe in God.   (8 marks)

Religious experience of many kinds may lead people to believe in God because what
they feel they experience is direct contact with God himself. They may believe they
have experienced God through prayer, meditation, a numinous experience, being
part of a corporate charismatic experience, or even a near-death experience. Some
people report a vision or a dream in which God communicates directly to them;
others may hear his voice during their everyday lives or in a more obviously religious
setting. A few may have a dramatic conversion experience, like that of the apostle
Paul. Others may feel the presence of God more quietly.

However, the most important point is that they feel they have met God personally
and are utterly convinced that he exists. The experience is so overwhelmingly real to
them that they are in no doubt that God is also real. They may feel that other explanations for the experience are no more likely than it being caused by God and they
may feel encouraged to do something for God as a result of the experience, to reflect
the effect it has had on them. Such an experience may not convince the person's
friends and family, because it is a personal thing, but for the believer who has met
God face to face it is the most convincing proof of all.

4

'The appearance of design and order in the world proves
that God exists.' Do you agree? Give reasons for your opinion,
showing you have considered another point of view.   (4 marks)

I agree with this claim. Along with many religious believers, I feel that the natural
world contains many features that can only be explained properly by belief in God.
The world appears to have been designed and all its parts seem to have been put
together for a purpose. For example, if God does not exist, why would the precise
conditions necessary for life on earth exist? Why would the planets move in perfect
rotation around the sun? Furthermore, the small details in a thumbprint or on a leaf
suggest that there must be a designer. For believers, that designer is God. Believers
may use the creation stories in Genesis or the Design Argument offered by William
Paley to support this view.

However, none of these features prove that God exists. What appears to be order
and design may be the result of pure chance or coincidence. Also, many features of

the world seem to go against the idea of design — earthquakes, floods and disease, for example. Moreover, how do we know that the universe *was* actually designed? We do not have another universe to compare it with.

Although the universe looks as if it is the kind of world God would have created, some people argue that is not enough evidence to prove that he does exist. All the features of the universe could be explained without God. Modern scientific advances show that living things in the world may have evolved into what they are now, and this process can happen without a designing God. Nevertheless, I believe that God is the explanation for these features.

Further questions

1 What is meant by the claim that God is omniscient? (2 marks)

2 What is meant by moral and natural evil? (2 marks)

3 Explain why evil and suffering are a problem for religious believers. (6 marks)

4 How might a religious experience bring a person to believe in God? (6 marks)

5 Describe the arguments for and against the view that miracles provide proof of the existence of God. (6 marks)

6 'Parents should let their children decide for themselves if God exists and should not try to influence them.' Do you agree? Give reasons for your opinion, showing you have considered another point of view. (4 marks)

Class activities and homework

Understanding why people believe in God

In pairs or small groups, draw a circle in the middle of a large sheet of paper. Write 'Religious experience' inside the circle. Around the outside, draw arrows. At the end of each arrow, name a different type of religious experience. Decide which of the experiences are the most convincing and which are the least convincing. Expand your diagram to include the reason for your decisions.

'Religious experiences are just hallucinations. They do not prove the existence of God.' Do you agree? Give reasons for your opinion, showing you have considered another point of view.

Understanding miracles

In pairs or small groups, divide a large sheet of paper into two columns. In the first column, list as many different types or examples of miracles as possible. In the second column, say whether or not there is a scientific explanation for what happened. Finally, look to see if any of the miracles have a non-religious explanation. Can any of the events be explained only by the existence and action of God? Under your teacher's guidance, share your views with the rest of the class.

'There is no such thing as miracles.' Do you agree? Give reasons for your opinion, showing you have considered another point of view.

Understanding the views of theists, atheists and agnostics

Your teacher will divide your class into three groups: theists, atheists and agnostics. Each group has a few minutes to make a list of the reasons supporting their viewpoint. Each group then elects a spokesperson to give their views to the other groups. When everyone has finished, each group may ask questions of the other groups, like a debate. At the end, the class should vote on which group has put forward the most convincing arguments.

Outline as many reasons as you can for people choosing not to believe in God and offer one argument against each of them. This will help you to develop your evaluation skills.

Understanding the problem of evil and suffering

In small groups, look at a copy of a recent newspaper. Find as many articles as you can about evil and suffering, and any articles that are about only good things. Discuss what caused the evil and suffering and how it could be resolved. In particular, think about what you would do if you were God.

Discuss how a religious believer might explain the problem of evil and suffering.

Matters of life and death

The sanctity of life

Christians and Muslims consider human life to be sacred. When something is sacred it is holy, which means it is set apart for God's purposes. This gives it a special value, beyond that of non-religious (**secular**) things. The **sanctity of life** arises from the belief that God created all life and it therefore belongs to him. Christians believe humans belong to God in a special way because they are made in his image.

Within Christianity, human life also has special value because God became human in the body of Jesus: 'The Word became flesh and lived among us' (John 1:14). Christians believe that life must be treated with special care. This is important when thinking about abortion, contraception, euthanasia, suicide, genetic engineering, medical treatment and technology.

Key words

Sanctity of life
The principle that life is sacred (holy) because God created it

Secular
A non-religious view, society or organisation

So God created man in his own image. In the image of God he created him: male and female, he created them.

(Genesis 1:27)

If we live, we live to the Lord: if we die, we die to the Lord. So whether we live or die, we belong to the Lord.

(Romans 14:8)

Both the birth and death of Jesus are important to Christians. For Jesus to die, and to take the punishment for humanity's sins, he had to be genuinely human: 'For God so loved the world that he gave his one and only Son, that whoever believes in him shall not perish but have eternal life' (John 3:16).

The birth of Jesus is important to Christians

For Christians, the human body is the place where the Holy Spirit dwells and is worthy of being treated with respect and honour: 'Your body is a temple of the Holy Spirit, who is in you, whom you have received from God. You are not on your own, therefore honour God with your body' (1 Corinthians 6:19–20). Some Christians make a decision not to smoke, abuse alcohol or take drugs for this reason. The view also influences beliefs about sexual behaviour — putting the body at risk from sexually trans-mitted diseases, for example — and even body piercing or tattoos, which are thought by some Christians to cheapen the value of the body.

Muslims share similar views, based on the belief that Allah created all human life and that he continues to be interested and involved in it. Birth is seen as a great gift from Allah and death as something that happens only according to his command.

Above all, for both Christians and Muslims, taking the life of another human being is wrong. Although it is not always avoidable — capital punishment is permitted in Islamic law and killing in war is inevitable in both Christian and Muslim cultures — the deliberate taking of life when there is a reason-able alternative not to do so poses hard questions which have to be answered. The commandment 'You shall not commit murder' (Exodus 20:13) means exactly that. In principle, Christians and Muslims teach that

Many people were concerned about the morality of the war in Iraq in 2004

God alone should have control over the beginning and the end of life. As the creator, only he has authority to bring it to an end.

> God alone is the Lord of life...no one can under any circumstances claim for himself the right directly to destroy an innocent human being.
>
> (Catechism of the Catholic Church)

Life after death

At the heart of most religious beliefs is the view that there will be an after-life that makes sense of the physical earthly life and in which its injustices will be balanced. For those who have been faithful to the teachings of their religion, the afterlife is something to be happily anticipated. Some believe that those who have not been faithful to God will face a less attractive existence in the afterlife.

Why do some people believe in life after death?

The prospect of an afterlife is attractive, not just for religious believers but for many people with no religious faith. People may believe in an afterlife for one or more of the following reasons:

- It is hard to believe that there is nothing beyond the life of the body. Humans somehow sense that they have a significance beyond their body and their earthly existence.
- Earthly life is often short, and in some cases cut off before people have fulfilled their potential. In an afterlife, this potential could be fulfilled.
- The moral law — people believe good should be rewarded and evil punished, but this does not always happen on earth. In an afterlife, God could ensure this was balanced out. People who have suffered greatly on earth may receive a reward in the afterlife. Surah 41:46 declares: 'Your good actions will benefit only you, while evil harms only the person who does it.' In other words, everything that people do in this life has implications for the afterlife and humans will be held personally accountable for their actions.
- The promise of an afterlife is in the Bible and the Qur'an and, if they are reliable and truthful documents, it is reasonable to believe that this afterlife will come about. Furthermore, if God created life to have purpose and significance, surely he would want that to continue beyond the grave. God's love for humanity and his desire to enter into a relationship with humans cannot be limited by the death of the human body.
- For Christians, the death and **resurrection** of Jesus are a special guarantee of life after death for all those who believe in him. Paul wrote: 'Now if Christ is proclaimed as raised from the dead, how can some of you say there is no resurrection of the dead?' (1 Corinthians 15:12).

Key word

Resurrection
The view that, after death, God recreates a new body in a heavenly place

Christianity and the afterlife

The belief that humans have a physical body and a spiritual soul is a form of **dualism** — the view that there are two parts to human nature. Other examples of dualism are dark and light, and good and evil. The two are contrasting and, in this case, the physical body is the part of human identity that decays; the spiritual soul is the part that endures even after death and goes to a spiritual realm, usually thought of within Christianity and Islam as **heaven**. The soul will be judged before God and will be held accountable for the person's earthly actions.

Teachings on what happens to the soul after this are varied. For some Christians, there are no easy answers. Those who have accepted Jesus as Lord and Saviour (sometimes referred to as having been 'born again'), and who have remained faithful to him throughout their lives, will enter into heaven and dwell eternally in the presence of God. Those who have not done so will go to **hell**, irrespective of how they have lived their lives or if they have lived obediently in accordance with any other religious faith. The traditional view of heaven is that it is a state of eternal happiness and peace with God. Hell is seen as a state of sorrow and regret without God.

However, this idea raises several problems. First, many modern Christians reject the idea of hell as a literal place, and especially as a place where there is eternal punishment and suffering. They claim that the notion of an all-loving God, who nevertheless will permit at least some of his creatures to enter such an appalling eternity, is unacceptable.

Another problem with the idea of life after death is whether the soul which lives on after the death of the physical body actually belonged to the same person before their body died. We are so used to identifying people by their physical appearance, how could we be certain that a soul after death could have the same personal identity as a body? Even if we do identify people by non-bodily characteristics (for example, we describe people as being kind, or having a good sense of humour), would those characteristics be identifiable without a body to convey them? After all, to be kind, we need vocal chords to express kind words, even if we do not perform any kind actions. We have no evidence for the existence of the soul as we do for the body, so it could simply be an idea.

Within Catholic teaching, a further idea is added — **purgatory**. This is a place where souls are purified to make them ready to enter into heaven.

Key words

Dualism
The view that there are two natures or sides to everything: a physical (seen) side and a spiritual (unseen) side

Heaven
A place where, after death, humans can live eternally in the presence of God. Other interpretations suggest that heaven is an *idea* in the minds of believers rather than an actual place

Hell
Traditionally, a place where unrepentant souls are eternally punished after death. Modern interpretations may refer to hell as the absence of God or even suggest that the evils of hell are experienced on earth rather than after death

Purgatory
The place where souls go after death to be purified for heaven

These are the souls of people who have committed sins which are serious, but not bad enough to separate them entirely from God's grace and love. People may pray for their loved ones in purgatory in the hope that their time there will be shortened. Protestant Christians do not accept the idea of purgatory.

> Those who have died in God's grace and are perfectly purified go to heaven. Those who have died in God's grace but were imperfectly purified [for example, Catholic sinners] will go to purgatory and be purified. Those who have refused to believe will go to hell. Then Jesus will come back to earth, the dead will be raised and all these souls will be reunited with their bodies. Then God will judge everyone. A new heaven and earth will be made and the resurrected from heaven will live there forever, but the resurrected from hell will return there forever.
>
> (Catechism of the Catholic Church)

Key word

Communion of saints
Christians who have died and gone to heaven, and who continue to be part of the Christian community on earth

The Last Judgement by Michelangelo

One idea shared by Catholics and some Protestants is the teaching on the **communion of saints**. This is the belief that Christians who have died and gone to heaven are still part of the Christian community, and Christians on earth can pray to Christians in heaven (the saints) for their help and guidance.

Another way of understanding the form the afterlife might take is a belief in the resurrection of the body. This suggests that after the death of a person's physical body, God will raise them to life again at the Day of Judgement. This will coincide with God's final judgement of the world and all people, living and dead. There are many different Christian ideas about when this will take place, and because there is no way of knowing when and if it will take place, much is based on speculation and interpretation of biblical texts that give only a limited amount of information. However, most Christians agree that it will in some way involve the resurrection to eternal life of those who have lived an earthly life of faith and devotion to God: 'God will give to each person according to what he has done. To those who by persistence in doing good seek glory, honour and immortality, he will give eternal life' (Romans 2:6–7).

The resurrection of Jesus is, of course, the strongest evidence given by Christians of bodily resurrection. Jesus appeared to his disciples after death, talked and ate with them, and they were able to touch him: 'Look at my hands and my feet. It is I myself! Touch me and see, a ghost does not have flesh and bones, as you see I have' (Luke 24:39). Paul also explains what the nature of the resurrected body will be: 'The body that is sown is perishable, it is raised imperishable…it is sown in a natural body, it is raised a spiritual body' (1 Corinthians 15:42–44). Although this idea is a popular one, there are several problems with it:

- If a person is resurrected, they are a replica of their earthly body. Is it really them or something that looks like them?
- Where is this place inhabited by resurrected bodies? Is it a physical place?
- Do people who have disabilities on earth still have them in heaven?
- If God recreates people after death, do they look the way they did at the moment of death or at some other point in their lives? If so, at what point? Do we have a choice?

Islam and the afterlife

Belief in akhira, or life after death, is an important part of the Muslim faith. In common with the Christian view of bodily resurrection, Muslims believe that after death the body will eventually be raised on the Day of Judgement, and where the afterlife is spent will depend on the outcome of that judgement. The angel of death takes the soul to barzakh, the waiting stage between the moment of death and the judgement, after which it will be sent to paradise (jannat) or to hell (janannam). On the Day of Judgement, two angels will open a book that contains a record of everyone's actions. If their name is on the right-hand side, they will be sent to jannat, but if it is on the left, they will go to janannam. Everyone will try to reach jannat by passing over the Assirat Bridge, but those destined for janannam will fall off.

Their status in Heaven and Hell may last for eternity, but this is subject to God's will and mercy.

(Surah 11:106–108)

Jannat is described in the Qur'an as a green garden, full of beautiful foliage and flowers and echoing with the sounds of birdsong and running water. Beautiful girls and wonderful food will be enjoyed there. On the other hand, janannam is a place of awful torment, fires, boiling water, scorching wind and black smoke. Those condemned to stay there are chained up to suffer eternal punishment.

We will not be prevented from changing your forms and creating you again in forms you know not.

(Surah 56:60–61)

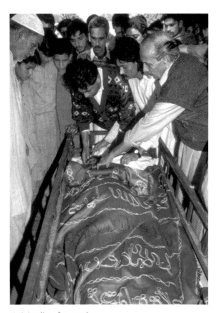

A Muslim funeral

Essentially, avoiding hell means following the Qur'an and the Shari'ah law (based on the Qur'an, the teachings of the Prophet Muhammad, and on the work of Islamic scholars), but some Muslims believe that non-Muslims who have led good lives may go to heaven. The way in which a Muslim lives his or her earthly life is constantly under scrutiny by Allah and will directly impact on their fate after death, as everything done or said is recorded. Muslims are always buried, never cremated, so the body is ready for resurrection. The afterlife is also the time in which good is rewarded and evil punished. Islam teaches that moral laws work on the principle of cause and effect, and those who deliberately do wrong must eventually face the consequences:

The unbelievers say, 'Never to us will come the hour.' But most surely, he may reward those who believe and work deeds of righteousness, for such is forgiveness and a sustenance most generous. But those who strive against our signs, to frustrate them, for such will be a chastisement, of painful wrath.

(Surah 34:3–5)

Once God's judgement has been passed, it cannot be changed:

> Until, when death comes to one of them, he says 'O, my Lord! Send me back to life, in order that I may work righteousness in the things I neglected.' The fire will burn their faces and they will therein grin with their lips displaced.

> (Surah 23:99–104)

Surah 56:15–21 teaches that those who live a good life will:

> sit on gold-encrusted thrones of happiness, reclining upon them, facing one another in [love]. Immortal youths will wait upon them with goblets, and ewers [urns], and cups filled with water from unsullied springs by which their minds will not be clouded and which will not make them drunk; and with fruit of any kind that they choose, and with flesh of any fowl that they may desire.

Other views on life after death

Near-death experiences

> [A near-death experience is] something very specific which can occur when people are near to death, or think themselves to be. It is not uncommon for people to have out of the ordinary experiences when they are in situations close to death.
> (Hugh Montefiore, *The Paranormal: A Bishop Investigates*, 2002)

In 1982, a poll found that 15% of those asked claimed to have had a near-death experience and a study of cardiac patients at Southampton Hospital found that 11% reported having had one. Scientific study has only become possible recently as more people have been resuscitated and been able to provide further evidence for these extraordinary experiences.

In a near-death experience, the people who have died describe a range of strange happenings:
- floating out of their bodies
- travelling down a tunnel into another world
- meeting Jesus, or a figure associated with their own religious tradition

- meeting a dead relative or friend
- facing a barrier or gate
- making a choice whether to cross the barrier or to return to earth

Although these experiences are very real to the person who has had them, they may not be reliable evidence for life after death. They could be caused by a lack of oxygen to the brain. Alternatively, they could be dreams or subconscious memories. It is certainly unlikely that a committed religious believer would accept evidence from a near-death or **paranormal** experience as proof of an afterlife.

Key word

Paranormal
Experiences that suggest there may be a non-visible, spirit world, for example ghosts or communications through mediums

The paranormal (parapsychology)

Some people believe there is a spirit world beyond the physical one, where spirits of the dead live on and can be contacted through a medium — someone who has the ability to communicate with the dead. Although many seances appear to be convincing, they are open to tremendous hoaxes and people who are grieving are easy targets for fraudulent mediums. The Old Testament expressly forbids people to become mediums: 'A man or woman who is a medium or spiritualist among you must be put to death' (Leviticus 20:27); and 1 Samuel 28 describes how Saul, the king of Israel, having asked the Witch of Endor to communicate with the spirit of the dead prophet Samuel, was told that as a punishment he would die in battle the following day. Committed Christians and Muslims would be cautious about engaging in such activities, which can be frightening and unpredictable.

Belief in ghosts and spirits is also not compatible with religious beliefs about the afterlife, although many people believe they do exist and are, in some way, evidence of an existence after death.

Why do some people not believe in life after death?

People do not necessarily reject a belief in the afterlife because they reject religious teaching about it. For some, it just does not seem reasonable that there is an afterlife, because there is no evidence for it. People may not believe there is an afterlife for one or more of the following reasons:

- If someone dies and has life after death as an **immortal soul** or a resurrected spiritual body, they are not the same person. What is the point of that?
- When people die, their bodies decay and nothing else happens to them.
- How can we be sure that an afterlife would be desirable?
- The idea of life after death is contradictory. A person is either dead or alive.

Abortion

Key words

Abortion
The termination of the life of a foetus in the womb

Immortal soul
A soul which can live on after the death of the physical body

An **abortion** is the termination of the life of a foetus in the womb. It may be called a surgical abortion, therapeutic abortion or termination, to clarify that it is carried out medically. A spontaneous or natural abortion is called a miscarriage.

Abortion is a difficult moral dilemma. The issue revolves around whether the foetus (sometimes referred to as the unborn child) is a human being. Those who claim it *is* may argue: 'It is wrong to take human life. A foetus is human life and therefore abortion is wrong.' Those who claim it is not may argue: 'It is wrong to take human life. However, a foetus is not a human life and therefore abortion is not wrong.'

It is difficult to say when human life begins. Is it at the moment:
- of fertilisation?
- when the fertilised egg is implanted into the wall of the womb?
- when movements of the foetus can be felt by the mother?
- when the foetus could, in principle, be capable of being born alive? This is called viability.
- of birth?

Abortion was illegal in the UK until 1967. This forced any woman who wanted an abortion to have an illegal termination, often in dangerous conditions, carried out by unqualified staff, at the risk to her own life and health. This led to great controversy. Supporters of legal abortions claimed that women who wanted them would always get them anyway, so legalising abortion would at least prevent them from facing additional risks and suffering.

As a result, abortions were made legal in the UK by the Abortion Act 1967 (amended in 1990), which allows abortion up to 24 weeks in pregnancy as long as two doctors agree on one of the following conditions:

- The mother's life is at risk.
- The mother's physical or mental health is at risk.
- The child might be born severely handicapped.
- There is a risk to the health of the mother's existing children.

Foetus at 20 weeks

Abortions are permitted later than 24 weeks' gestation if the mother's life is at risk, but for no other reason. There are about 180,000 legal abortions in the UK every year and most are carried out within the first 12 weeks of pregnancy.

The abortion law is likely to face changes in the near future. People in favour of the woman's right to choose whether or not to have a termination (pro-choice supporters) face opposition from those who oppose abortion largely on the grounds that the right to life is the most important factor (pro-life supporters). Many pro-life supporters believe 24 weeks is far too late. As a result of developments in neo-natal care, very premature babies have a much greater chance of survival than used to be the case and a baby born at 24 weeks is now much more likely to survive, so it seems wrong to abort foetuses at this late stage. It is likely that a reduction to 18 weeks' gestation may be legalised at some time in the future.

Arguments in favour of abortion

The woman's right to choose

Supporters of the woman's right to choose whether to abort claim that the decision affects five important areas of her life, which only she should be able to control:

- her future
- her relationships
- whether to have a child

- what happens to her body
- what happens to her life

In some cases, there may also be an argument based on compassion, if having the child would cause great hardship. Abortion gives the woman the chance to make choices about her fertility, taking into account all the factors that will affect her, her child, and possibly her partner or existing children. In all cases, the pro-choice supporter will argue that the rights of the mother are greater than those of the foetus since the foetus is not able to survive outside the mother's womb.

Pro-choice supporters campaign against reform of the abortion law

Quality of life

This argument takes into account the actual life the foetus is likely to have after birth. If the child is likely to suffer great pain and hardship, the principle of the sanctity of life may take second place to the quality of life the child will have. The case of Charlotte Wyatt, who was born when her mother was 26 weeks pregnant, raised considerable public and media interest when a judge supported a hospital's advice not to continue resuscitating her. Charlotte had multiple internal organ damage, was blind and unable to communicate, and was said to be suffering great pain. Her parents wanted to wait to see if God would intervene miraculously, but the hospital felt the baby's best interests were not being served by resuscitating her.

Population growth

Some politicians have argued that abortion acts as a form of population control in countries such as Brazil, where there is already great hardship resulting from poverty and overcrowding. Some countries, such as China in the 1970s and 1980s, placed financial penalties on families with more than one child, and in such cases abortion was considered not only acceptable but an obligation.

Arguments against abortion

Pro-life or anti-abortionist groups, such as LIFE and the Society for the Protection of the Unborn Child, claim that the rights of the foetus as a human being are the most important. Pro-life supporters claim that the suggestion that some babies are better off not being born, or that they would interfere in the mother's other plans, is wrong. In the pro-choice debate,

Pro-life supporters campaign against abortion

the child in the womb is generally referred to as the 'foetus' rather than the 'baby'. Anti-abortionists say doctors use this language because 'terminating the foetus' does not sound as bad as 'killing the baby'.

Pro-life supporters argue that the foetus has a right:
- to fulfil its potential
- for its life to be valued
- not to be killed
- to be fairly represented by an unbiased third party (i.e. not the mother or father)

Key word

Contraception
A range of methods that may be used to prevent conception

Pro-life groups may also express grave concern over the methods used for abortion. The controversial 'abortion pill', which requires no surgical procedure, has made abortion easier to obtain and to carry out, and increases the likelihood of abortion being seen as a form of **contraception**.

The religious viewpoint

Christian teaching on abortion

Within Christianity, most Roman Catholics are opposed to abortion. They may offer a range of arguments, including:
- every human being has the right to life
- abortion is murder
- life is a sacred gift from God and only he can end a pregnancy
- the unborn child is created in the image of God

- God has a plan for every human life: 'For you created my innermost being: you knit me together in my mother's womb' (Psalm 139:13)
- life begins at the moment of conception

> Abortion is a horrible crime...the law must provide appropriate sanctions for every deliberate violation of the child's rights.
>
> (Catechism of the Catholic Church)

The Church of England and the Methodist Church are more liberal on the issue. They agree that abortion is undesirable but believe it may, under some circumstances, be the lesser of two evils and the most loving thing to do, perhaps in cases of rape or when the life of the mother is at risk.

> We also believe that to withdraw compassion in circumstances of extreme distress or need is a very great evil. In an imperfect world the 'right' choice is sometimes the lesser of two evils.
>
> (Church of England)

> In an imperfect world there will be circumstances where termination of a pregnancy may be the lesser of two evils.
>
> (Methodist Church)

In reaching their conclusion, they may take these points into account:
- Jesus taught his followers to act with a spirit of love and compassion. Sticking to a rigid rule against abortion in all circumstances may be unloving to both mother and child.
- The sanctity of life is broken in some cases and this is supported by religion, for example in times of war.
- It is by no means certain that life begins at conception.
- Medical technology has advanced so that handicapped foetuses can be identified quickly. This means earlier, quicker, less drastic abortions can take place with fewer side effects for the mother.

Islamic teaching on abortion

Within Islam, abortion is permitted only if the mother's life is at risk, when it is considered the lesser of two evils. Some Muslims claim abortion is permissible before 120 days on the grounds that the soul does not enter the body before that date. Others argue that it is impossible to say anything with certainty about the soul, and so, from the moment of conception, the life of the foetus should be protected. In pre-Islamic Arabia, unwanted newborns — especially girls — were buried face down in the sand to suffocate and as a result this practice was expressly forbidden in the Qur'an: 'Slay not your children...the killing of them is a great sin' (Surah 17:31). Lack of resources is also not considered a justifiable reason for abortion: 'Do not slay your children because of poverty — we will provide for you and for them' (Surah 6:151). The Qur'an states too that aborted babies will call their mothers to account on Judgement Day: 'When the souls are sorted out, when the female infant buried alive is asked for what crime she was killed...when the world on high is unveiled...then shall each soul know what it has sent ahead' (Surah 81:7–9, 11, 14).

Euthanasia

Euthanasia is the intentional killing by act or omission, of one whose life is deemed not worth living.

(*New Dictionary of Christian Ethics and Pastoral Theology*, 1995)

Key word

Euthanasia
Literally a 'good' or 'happy' death; usually refers to mercy killing or prematurely ending the life of a terminally ill patient

The term '**euthanasia**' is based on the Greek terms *eu-thanatos* and defined in the *Oxford English Dictionary* as referring to a 'good' or 'happy' death. In our context, it is used to refer to the deliberate bringing about of a 'good' death, often described as a mercy killing. In recent years, sympathy towards euthanasia has risen, especially in the Netherlands.

Most debates about euthanasia revolve around **voluntary euthanasia** — mercy killing carried out at the express wish of the patient. However, there are four other types of euthanasia:

- **Active euthanasia**: the result of positive action (e.g. lethal injection) on the part of a carer, usually a medical professional.
- **Passive euthanasia**: the termination of treatment that is prolonging the patient's life. This is already carried out in the case of severely damaged newborn babies (see page 37), and may apply to withdrawal of life support from a patient in a coma. Patients may legitimately give instructions not to be resuscitated in the case of a heart attack or other immediate threat to their life. Such instructions include living wills

or advance directives, whereby patients indicate that, should they become severely injured or handicapped, they wish to be allowed to die rather than to receive intensive medical treatment. Although doctors are not obliged to honour these instructions, they may choose to do so out of respect or compassion.

- **Involuntary euthanasia**: carried out without the express permission of the patient.
- **Assisted suicide**: the provision of the means and/or the opportunity whereby a patient may terminate their life themselves.

Key words

Active euthanasia
Taking active steps to end the life of a patient, for example by giving a lethal injection

Assisted suicide
The provision of means and/or opportunity whereby a patient may terminate their life themselves

Involuntary euthanasia
Ending the life of a patient who is not able to make the request for themselves

Passive euthanasia
Withdrawing medical treatment or nourishment to hasten the death of a patient

Voluntary euthanasia
Ending the life of a patient at their request

Arguments in favour of euthanasia

Those who support euthanasia may offer the following reasons:
- It allows the patient a gentle, pain-free death.
- It permits the patient to die with dignity, rather than suffer a slow death after facing increasing mental and physical deterioration.
- It saves on hospital and medical expenses and frees beds for non-terminal patients.
- It relieves the emotional and financial burden on families.

Those who support the legalisation of euthanasia argue that if humans did not fear death so much, they might be more able to see euthanasia as something positive and humane, not something to be afraid of.

> Even though human death is an evil to be fought against, and a reality which can never be sought intentionally, it may also at times be accepted, even welcomed, as a sign of God's mercy.
>
> (John Wyatt, *Matters of Life and Death*, 1998)

Under strictly controlled conditions, euthanasia has been made legal in some countries, including the Netherlands and Switzerland. There have been cases in which UK citizens have travelled abroad to obtain euthanasia.

The level of medical care that can now be offered to terminally sick patients has become a problem. Medical technology can keep people alive for much longer, but their quality of life may be poor, and they may do little but drift in and out of consciousness. Huge doses of painkillers may be needed which, ultimately, may kill them anyway. Sometimes this is done deliberately. Such treatment is an example of double effect, whereby the primary purpose of the painkillers is to relieve pain but the secondary effect is that the patient dies of an overdose.

In 1993, the House of Lords rejected a proposal to legalise euthanasia, saying: 'It would be next to impossible to ensure that all acts of euthanasia were truly voluntary.'

Arguments against euthanasia

Arguments against euthanasia focus on the problem of the so-called 'slippery slope' — the fear that once euthanasia became legal, it would be impossible to stop it. This would put enormous pressure on the sick and dying. Patients in a persistent vegetative state have been known to recover and illnesses diagnosed as 'terminal' do not always end in death. However, if euthanasia were easily available, a decision to die could be taken far too quickly. It is also not necessarily the case that terminal patients have to suffer a painful, undignified death. The hospice movement aims to care for the terminally sick, placing the emphasis on palliative care (pain relief). They work to help doctors and the general public understand that there are alternatives to euthanasia. However, at present, hospice care is expensive and limited. It is claimed that not enough medical professionals are interested in palliative care to make it a priority; it is not as obviously glamorous as many other healthcare specialities.

> We are now always able to control pain in terminal cancer in the patients sent to us...euthanasia as advocated is wrong...it should be unnecessary and is an admission of defeat.
>
> (Christian Hospice Movement)

Joni Eareckson Tada, a Christian quadriplegic who campaigns for the rights of the disabled, wrote a powerful book called *When Is It Right to Die?* (1992). In it, she writes:

> I once cornered Dr J. L. Packer, a prominent evangelical theologian, and asked him this question: 'What would you suggest to a severely handicapped man with cerebral palsy who was totally bedridden, non-verbal, and relegated to a back bedroom in a nursing home? No one visits him and no nurse takes time to benefit from his good attitude. What can that handicapped man do?'…Dr Packer replied, 'A man like that can worship and glorify God.'

The religious viewpoint

Christian teaching on euthanasia

Like abortion, euthanasia involves the issue of the sanctity of life. Some Christian denominations agree that doctors should have the right to switch off life-support machines with the consent of the patient's family. However, the Roman Catholic Church teaches that it is wrong to take any action to kill a patient or to fail to take action that would help them to survive, even if the action, or omission of action, is intended to relieve suffering: 'An act or omission which causes death in order to eliminate suffering constitutes a murder greatly contrary to the dignity of the human person and to the respect due to the living God, his Creator' (Catechism of the Catholic Church).

Islamic teaching on euthanasia

The Muslim view, like that of Christianity, is that all types of euthanasia are forbidden, based on the principle of maqasid ash-Sharia'ah — the preservation of life. Euthanasia is also opposed to hifdh ad-din — keeping religious principles permanent — because it asserts human, rather than divine, authority over life and encourages murder and suicide. Even living wills are considered dubious. Since life belongs to Allah alone, it is open to question whether the individual has the right to make this decision. The principle of injury (darar) claims that no one should be hurt or cause hurt to others, and yet euthanasia cannot fail to cause some degree of pain and suffering.

Although the principle of hardship (mashaqqah) permits the law to be relaxed in some circumstances in order to relieve suffering, Muslim legal specialists do not include the pain and suffering of terminal illness among them. However, continuing medical treatment is not obligatory if a terminal illness is causing unbearable hardship and withdrawal of treatment is done to relieve the patient and their family.

Within Islam, all suffering is a test. Who is to know what plans Allah has for an individual and the suffering they are enduring? His plans are far greater than our human attempts to avoid difficulties and trials. To reject Allah's tests and trials could have serious implications for a person's place in the afterlife.

Developments in right to die laws

Towards the end of 2004 important steps were being taken to make it easier for terminally and chronically ill patients to pursue the legal right to die. On 30 November 2004, the High Court lifted an order banning a man, identified only as Mr Z, from taking his chronically ill wife to Switzerland for an assisted suicide. This was a legal milestone, which led the chief executive of the Voluntary Euthanasia Society to say: 'This is a very important judgement, a watershed. It means that the Suicide Act is on its last legs'. The ruling may set a precedent which would protect relatives and friends who helped suffering loved ones to die from prosecution.

In December 2004 Parliament addressed the Mental Capacity Bill which is an attempt to clarify the law over the treatment of the dying. If passed by Parliament, this would give legal force to living wills or advance directives in which people could express a wish in advance to have life-prolonging treatment withheld if they became severely incapacitated. It would also provide for individuals to give power of attorney to relatives or friends to make decisions on their behalf and give doctors the right to challenge them, in court if necessary, if they disagreed. The continuing concern is that living wills could be made hastily by patients or their representatives, based on a casual conversation or for unworthy motives.

Questions and activities

Sample questions and answers

1 What is meant by the term 'abortion'?   (2 marks)

An abortion is the termination of the life of a foetus in the womb before it is carried to full term.

2 Outline the reasons for not believing in life after death. (6 marks)

For some people, life after death is not a desirable prospect; for others, the evidence of the senses tells them that when someone dies, their body decays and nothing seems to live on. Some people go further and claim that the very idea of life after death is a logical impossibility anyway — if you are dead, you cannot have life again. Furthermore, some reject the idea of life after death because, they claim, anything that lives on after death is not the dead person — their personal identity ended with the death of the body. A resurrected version of them is simply a replica; although they may look the same, they are not the same person. There is little evidence that is strong enough to convince people of the existence of an afterlife. Accounts of near-death experiences can be explained easily in other ways, and mediums who claim to be able to communicate with the dead are often revealed to be fraudulent. Some people may also claim that the only reason to believe in an afterlife is because people are afraid of death, and it is nothing more than a psychologically comforting thought with no reality. Above all, if God does not exist, the notion of life after death, including ideas of reward and punishment, are meaningless. If God does not exist, who can bring about such an after-death existence? It is clearly beyond human ability, so it is not even worthwhile discussing it.

3 Explain why Christians have different views concerning abortion. (8 marks)

The main reason why many Christians, especially those within the Roman Catholic and Evangelical Churches, are opposed to abortion is because they believe that the unborn foetus is a human being from the moment of conception. For them, it follows that to abort a foetus is to kill a human being. This is forbidden in the Bible: 'Do not commit murder' (Exodus 20:13). Abortion also violates the notion of the sanctity of life — life is a sacred gift from God and only he can take it away. To perform an abortion is to go against the will of God. The unborn child, many Christians claim, is created in the image of God and has human rights, including the right to live. The Catechism of the Catholic Church states: 'God alone is the Lord of life…no one can, under any circumstances, claim for himself the right directly to destroy an innocent human being.'

However, some Christians are prepared to be more flexible because they recognise that there are times when it is more compassionate to allow an abortion than to insist on a continuation of the pregnancy. If a woman's life is in danger, it may be

possible to apply the principle of double effect, which justifies performing an abortion if the primary purpose is to save the mother's life, not to kill the foetus. Some Christians may also argue that if the pregnancy is due to rape or incest, or if the baby is likely to be seriously handicapped, the woman should be allowed an abortion on compassionate grounds. Christians who hold these views may, however, find themselves facing considerable opposition from more conservative Christian groups.

4 'Euthanasia can never be right.' Do you agree? Give reasons for your opinion, showing you have considered another point of view. In your answer, you should refer to at least one religion.

(4 marks)

Euthanasia is the deliberate killing of someone who is suffering very serious illness or handicap. Christians might say euthanasia is always wrong because the Bible says people should not kill each other as God has created everyone. This is called the sanctity of life. However, many people argue that euthanasia may, at times, be a good thing, especially if the person involved is very old or suffering a great deal without hope of getting better. The person concerned may want to die to end their suffering, and also the suffering of their families and friends who care for them. Those who are against euthanasia say it is the job of doctors to save life, not take it. Moreover, people who have been diagnosed as being seriously handicapped or terminally ill *have* recovered. The 'slippery slope' argument — which says that, if euthanasia were available, pressure would be put on people to die — is a powerful one. On the other hand, supporters of euthanasia say a gentle, dignified death is preferable to a slow death through pain and suffering. They also argue that euthanasia will save valuable hospital and medical resources.

I believe that it cannot be true that euthanasia is 'never' right. Because everyone is in a different situation, there may be times when it is right and times when it is not. It must be judged according to people's individual circumstances, and their own religious beliefs should be taken into account even if they cannot speak for themselves.

Further questions

1 What is meant by the term 'voluntary euthanasia'?   (2 marks)

2 What is a near-death experience?   (2 marks)

3 Explain what Christianity (or Islam) understands by the sanctity of life.   (6 marks)

4 Outline Christian (or Muslim) beliefs concerning life after death.   (6 marks)

5 Explain two differing Christian beliefs about what happens after death.   (8 marks)

6 'Religion provides the best preparation for death.' Do you agree?
   Give reasons for your opinion, showing you have considered another
   point of view.   (4 marks)

Class activities and homework

Understanding life after death

Read Revelation 20:11–15. This gives a graphic description of the events at the end of time. Discuss and evaluate the difficulties presented by this kind of material. Find similar descriptions in the Qur'an. What are the similarities and differences?

'Belief in life after death is absolutely central to religious believers. If there is no afterlife, their faith is meaningless.' Do you agree? Give reasons for your opinion, showing you have considered another point of view.

Understanding abortion

Your teacher will divide your class into two groups. One group will represent the pro-life movement, and the other the pro-choice lobby. Choose a motion, for example: 'This house considers that abortion should be illegal under all circumstances.' Choose a proposer and a seconder for your group. With your teacher acting as chairperson, conduct a debate on the motion.

There are some interesting anti-abortion websites. Use a search engine to carry out an internet search to see what you can find. Be critically evaluative of the methods the websites use to convey their message. Do you think they are effective?

Understanding euthanasia

Christians believe this life is lived from the perspective of the next, and decisions made about it should be made in the context of mankind's relationship with God. In the light of this, discuss the following quotations:

- The influential Evangelical Christian, Joni Eareckson Tada, herself a quadriplegic, writes:

> God knows you're heading for a hereafter. For those who, apart from him, prematurely end their lives hoping to find relief, there will only be a hereafter of vast and utter disappointment. For those who believe in Jesus, the dying process becomes the most significant passage of their lives.
>
> (Joni Eareckson Tada, *When Is It Right to Die?*, 1992)

- Consider this alternative view as expressed by Friedrich Nietzsche:

> In a certain state it is indecent to live longer. To go on vegetating in cowardly dependence on physicians and machinations, after the meaning of life, the right to life, has been lost, that ought to prompt a profound contempt in society…I want to die proudly when it is no longer possible to live proudly.
>
> (Quoted in John Wyatt, *Matters of Life and Death*, 1998)

Find out more about hospices by looking at some of their websites. Begin with www.stchristophers.org.uk. Think about the way they describe themselves and their aims. Do you think the hospice sounds like a good place to live with a terminal illness? In the light of these thoughts, discuss the following claim:

> Human life span is limited, not just as a curse, but out of God's grace…. Even though human death is an evil to be fought against, and a reality which can never be sought intentionally, it may also at times be accepted, even welcomed, as a sign of God's mercy.
>
> (John Wyatt, *Matters of Life and Death*, 1998)

Section 3

Marriage and the family

Sexual relationships

The Christian viewpoint

The view of the Christian Church is that sex should be restricted to marriage and that marriage should be for life. Therefore, it claims that sex before marriage and **adultery** are wrong and that married couples should show **faithfulness** to each other. **Promiscuity** (having casual sexual relationships), **pre-marital sex** (having sex before you are married) and adultery (when a married person has sex with someone other than their husband or wife) are considered by most Christians to be wrong.

Key words

Adultery
Having a sexual relationship with someone other than your marriage partner

Faithfulness
Maintaining a sexual relationship with the same person

Pre-marital sex
Sexual intercourse prior to marriage

Promiscuity
A lifestyle characterised by casual sexual relationships

> You shall not commit adultery.   (Exodus 20:14)

> God wants you to be holy and completely free from sexual immorality.
>
> (1 Thessalonians 4:3)

Many Christians believe that sex should only take place within a marriage relationship. The reasons for this are:

- The Bible is critical of non-marital sexual relationships.
- Children born outside marriage may have a less stable family life.
- Unprotected sex outside marriage makes people vulnerable to sexually transmitted diseases.
- Sexual union unites a married couple.

> The sexual act must take place exclusively within marriage. Outside marriage it always constitutes a grave sin.
>
> (Catechism of the Catholic Church)

Key word

Divorce
The legal termination of a marriage

However, some Christians believe sex before marriage is right if the couple love each other and they are in a long-term relationship that they intend will lead to marriage. Indeed, many Christians today believe the teaching of the Church on marriage is old-fashioned and ought to be modernised. In particular, some have objected to forbidding sex before marriage and the requirement that marriage should be for life, which can cause misery if the relationship does not work. Some think that it is wrong for the Church to force people to remain in a marriage that brings pain and suffering. Some Christians going through separation and **divorce** have suffered harsh treatment from their Church at the very time they need to be treated with kindness.

The Islamic viewpoint

> Nor come nigh to adultery for it is a shameful deed and an evil opening the road to other evils.
>
> (Surah 17:32)

Islam offers equally important teachings on non-marital sexual relationships. In an attempt to prevent pre-marital sex, girls and boys are often separated during puberty and great modesty is encouraged in dress and behaviour.

Some Muslim girls prefer not to travel unaccompanied with a man who is not a family member. Muslim teaching on relationships between the sexes has an impact on all aspects of social life, education and the work place. Many Muslim girls and women wear coverings — sometimes on the head, sometimes over the whole body — to preserve their integrity outside the home. Interestingly, many women say that wearing hijab makes them feel more, not less, free, as they are not worried about being seen as objects of sexual attraction.

Muslim girls are encouraged to dress modestly

Say to the believing men that they should lower their gaze and guard their modesty: that will make for greater purity for them: and Allah is well acquainted with all that they do.

(Surah 24:30)

Those who are unable to marry are encouraged to fast (go without food) to curb their sexual appetites. Yusuf Abdulah Al-Qaradawi observes:

When Islam prohibits something, it closes all the avenues leading to it. This is achieved by prohibiting every step and every means leading to that which is haram [not permitted]. Accordingly, whatever excites passions, opens ways for illicit sexual relations between a man and woman and promotes indecency and obscenity is haram.

(www.islamonline.net)

Al-Qaradawi adds:

Islam is very strict in prohibiting zina [adultery], for it leads to confusion of lineage, child abuse, the break-up of families, bitterness in relationships, the spread of venereal diseases, and a general laxity in morals.

The Qur'an teaches avoidance, as far as is possible, of sexual immorality of all kinds:

> And say to the believing women that they should. . . draw their veils over their bosoms, and not display their beauty except to their husbands' sons, their brothers or their brothers' sons, or their sisters' sons, or their womenfolk.
>
> (Surah 24:31)

Contraception

Contraception is the deliberate prevention of pregnancy. It involves using one of a number of methods, including the pill, the morning-after pill, condoms, the diaphragm (cap), the IUD (coil), sterilisation and vasectomy.

Christian teaching on contraception

Many Christians believe every act of sexual intercourse should be open to the possibility of conception. They argue that using artificial methods of contraception is wrong because they prevent humans fulfilling God's command to 'Be fruitful and multiply' (Genesis 1:28). Therefore, only a natural method of contraception should be used, planning love making around the woman's menstrual cycle and attempting to predict the times in the cycle when she is not likely to conceive.

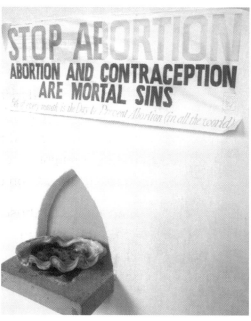

Protestant Christians consider that, within a marriage relationship, contraception can be used to plan and manage a family. For most, a barrier method such as the cap or condom is acceptable, since the sperm and egg are prevented from meeting and so conception cannot take place. However, for many Christians, the coil and the morning-after pill, which act after conception

Many Roman Catholics are opposed to contraception and abortion to prevent implantation, are considered to be the equivalent to an abortion and are therefore unacceptable. The conventional pill, which prevents conception, is acceptable.

Islamic teaching on contraception

Some Muslims are against contraception. Others maintain that, if the mother's life or health would be at risk if she became pregnant, or if the family — existing children or the new child — would suffer materially or physically, then its use is justifiable. In such cases, contraception should not be considered as drastic as abortion or open to the same criticisms.

Cohabitation

In the UK today, about half of all couples choose to live together without being married. This is called **cohabitation**. Some couples choose to live together before marriage, while others live together instead of getting married. The arguments in favour of cohabitation are that it enables couples to get to know each other properly before making the commitment of marriage and that, if the relationship does not work, they can separate without the legal problems of divorce.

> **Key word**
>
> **Cohabitation**
> A man and woman living together as a married couple without legalising their union through marriage

Some people argue against cohabitation, claiming it encourages a casual and selfish attitude towards relationships. It is too easy to break up and so couples are not encouraged to talk things through when times get tough. In particular, those against cohabitation say children are best brought up in a stable home with two married parents. However, with increasing numbers of children being brought up perfectly successfully by cohabiting parents, this is a more difficult position to maintain.

An increasing number of Christians today believe they should be allowed to cohabit, perhaps as a trial marriage. In this way, they can develop a better relationship with their partner and one that is more likely to last a lifetime. In 1995, the Church of England published a report called *Something to Celebrate* which said that couples who are cohabiting should be acceptable to the Church, and that cohabitation could be seen as a step towards a final commitment to marriage.

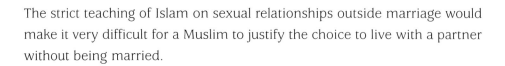
The strict teaching of Islam on sexual relationships outside marriage would make it very difficult for a Muslim to justify the choice to live with a partner without being married.

Marriage

Perhaps the most important way to show love is through marriage. Although marriage is a legal state, it carries great significance within virtually all the world religions. Marriage is the lifelong union of two people that can only be ended by the death of one partner or by divorce. Most people are attracted to a member of the opposite sex and fall in love. They find themselves personally attracted to each other, talking together and sharing each other's interests. They usually also share physical attraction and sexual union. Moreover, the couple need to respect, value and support each other.

Key word

Bigamy
Getting married while still married legally to someone else

Marriage is also a legal commitment. In the UK, there are four legal requirements that must be fulfilled before a marriage can take place:

- The couple must be male and female (homosexual marriages are not recognised in the UK).
- Both partners must be over 16 years old (and, if under 18 years, have their parents' consent).
- Neither partner must be already married to someone else (this is called **bigamy**).
- Both partners must enter into the marriage freely, not under threat.

The civil marriage ceremony

About 250,000 couples marry in the UK each year. About half of these marriages take place in a church; the rest are usually civil marriage ceremonies. A civil ceremony is normally smaller and less grand than a church wedding and is performed by a registrar, who is a civil servant. There are usually fewer guests and there is no religious element in the ceremony. The registrar asks if there is any reason why the couple should not marry each other, then the couple exchange rings and make vows promising to live together in whatever circumstances until death. The couple sign a legal document and are officially married.

Civil weddings need not take place in a registrar's office. They can be held anywhere that is licensed for weddings. This means that couples may choose to be married virtually anywhere they wish and civil weddings are becoming as glamorous as traditional church weddings.

Christian teaching on marriage

The Christian view of marriage is that it is a gift from God. The man and the woman make a commitment to each other to live together in an exclusive, loving relationship until the death of one of the partners. This is called faithfulness — promising to have sexual relations only with the marriage partner. The Bible shows that marriage was part of God's plan for humanity: 'For this reason, a man will leave his father and mother and be united to his wife, and they will become one flesh' (Genesis 2:24). Marriage also provides a stable and secure environment into which children can be born and raised. Marriage is the basis of the family and, in turn, the family is the basis of society itself.

The Bible's teaching on some aspects of married life is controversial today. It says that there is an order within the marriage relationship, in which the husband is the head over the wife. The husband must love and honour his wife and she, in turn, is to respect and honour him: 'Wives, submit to your husbands as to the Lord. For the husband is the head of the wife as Christ is the head of the Church.... Husbands, love your wives, just as Christ loved the Church' (Ephesians 5:22–25).

This teaching may seem old-fashioned in a society in which men and women are equals. Most Christians suggest it means a truly loving husband would carry the responsibility of authority in the way that Jesus did — to help, protect and encourage his wife. However, in an era when many women earn more than their husbands, and have often lived independent, successful

Key word

Equality
Treating people in
the same way
irrespective of sex,
race, education,
disability or any
other factor that
may set them
apart

single lives before marriage, much negotiation needs to take place to come to an agreed understanding of what this teaching means for their marriage relationship.

In other respects, the Bible teaches that marriage is a union of equals: 'The wife's body does not belong to her alone but also to her husband. In the same way, the husband's body does not belong to him alone but also to his wife' (1 Corinthians 7:4). **Equality** means the wife and the husband can have different roles, drawing on their respective personal strengths rather than assuming that the husband must do some tasks (control finances, for example) and the wife others (for example, cooking).

The Christian marriage ceremony

Many Christians regard marriage as a sacrament — this means it is a ceremony in which the Church conveys God's love and grace to believers. The opening words of the marriage service in the Church of England clearly show what the commitment of marriage is all about:

> Marriage is given that husband and wife may comfort and help each other, living faithfully together in need and in plenty, in sorrow and in joy…it is given that they may have children and be blessed in caring for them and bringing them up in accordance with God's will.

The wedding ceremony includes the following features, promises and acts of worship:
- The couple exchange vows, committing themselves to each other.
- They exchange rings as a sign of the everlasting nature of their relationship.
- The priest prays for God's blessing and help in their relationship.
- Prayers are said for the couple. Sometimes they take their first holy communion as husband and wife.

The vows the couple make to each other are at the very centre of the ceremony. Vows are solemn promises made before God and the guests, which, ideally, should not be broken. Most Christian ceremonies use similar vows. These are the vows used in the Roman Catholic service:

3

I call upon the persons here to witness that I [name], do take you [name] to be my lawful wedded [wife/husband], to have and to hold from this day forward, for better, for worse, for richer, for poorer, in sickness and in health, to love and to cherish, till death us do part.

Each of the vows is a different promise. 'For better, for worse, for richer, for poorer' is about faithfulness — the partner will stay faithful and not leave the other because times are difficult or not what they had hoped them to be. 'In sickness and in health' is about loyalty — the partner will be there for the other, not only in times of health, but also when they are sick. Finally, the vow 'to love and to cherish' is about caring — the partner should love the other and make them feel really special, never taking them for granted.

A traditional church wedding

Islamic teaching on marriage

The ideal marriage partner is one whose love for God singles him or her out as a true Muslim and the Prophet Muhammad is reported to have said: 'If someone whose faith and morals you trust makes a proposal of marriage to you, then marry him, otherwise there will be trials and much corruption in the land' (www.islamonline.net).

Islam views marriage as a contract that requires the full consent of the parties concerned. While third parties, including parents, may give advice, the final decision must be a free choice on the part of each partner. However, the Qur'an acknowledges that the right of women to make a free choice may not be recognised: 'O ye who believe! Ye are forbidden to inherit women against their will' (Surah 4:19). Any adult man or woman can arrange their own marriage contract, which involves a gift from the husband to the wife and a commitment from each party to make life physically, emotionally and spiritually comfortable for each other. The responsibility for taking care of economic needs usually falls to the man. The greater responsibility that men have as protectors and providers gives them the greater right in making decisions.

Key words

Monogamy
Being married to only one person

Polygamy
Being married to more than one person at the same time

Although in the West most Muslims choose their own marriage partners, some Muslim marriages are arranged by the couple's parents. Most Muslims marry within their faith, and marriage is encouraged at a young age. Some followers accept **polygamy** (more than one marriage partner), although **monogamy** is generally considered to be the norm. Polygamy, if practised, should be carried out under strict conditions, and the existing wife must give her consent to her husband taking another bride. He may do so if he feels that he will be helping a widow or showing a woman kindness in some way by offering her marriage. The maximum number of wives a man can have is four. In the UK, it is illegal to have more than one spouse.

> Marry women of your choice, two or three or four; but if ye fear that ye shall not be able to deal justly with them, only one.
>
> (Surah 4:3)

The Muslim marriage ceremony

A Muslim marriage ceremony

There are four key features of a Muslim wedding ceremony:

- The couple declare before witnesses that they are freely entering into the marriage.
- A contract is signed, which guarantees that if the wife leaves her husband, the marriage gift she received from him (the mahr) will still belong to her.
- The imam reads from the Qur'an, offers prayers and a says a khutbah (sermon).
- The marriage is celebrated publicly with a feast.

To marry or remain single?

It is worth noting that Christians do not have to marry. It is not a command of God and, indeed, some may feel they can serve God better if they are not married.

It is expected, however, that all Muslims will marry. This is because the Prophet Muhammad was married, and so marriage is sunnah. Marriage raises the value of a person's prayers, and brings God's power, blessing and forgiveness. Sexual desire is a creative gift from God and cannot, in itself, be seen as evil. Men and women, therefore, are encouraged through marriage to fulfil that desire and to have children.

Wasa'il'sh-Shiah relates the following episode from the Prophet's life:

> A woman came to the Prophet's house and her strong perfume soon filled the house. When the Prophet inquired about the visitor, the woman said that she had tried everything to attract her husband, but in vain; he does not leave his meditation to pay any attention to her. The Prophet told her to inform her husband about the reward of sexual intercourse, which he described as follows: 'When a man approaches his wife, he is guarded by two angels and at that moment in Allah's views he is like a warrior fighting for the cause of Allah. When he has intercourse with her, his sins fall like the leaves of the tree in autumn.'
>
> (Quoted on www.al-islam.org)

Divorce

> That which God has joined together, let no one divide.
>
> (Church of England service book)

A divorce is the legal termination of a marriage. In the UK, the law allows divorce if the marriage has 'irretrievably broken down'. This may have a number of causes, but the most common are adultery, unreasonable behaviour and desertion. Today, approximately a third of all marriages end in divorce and there are about 160,000 divorces each year in the UK.

The number of divorces is rising every year. There are several reasons for this:
- Divorce is easier and cheaper to obtain than it was even 40 years ago.
- Women and men are less prepared to put up with bad treatment from their partners than they used to be.
- Divorce does not carry the social stigma that it did in the past.

Those who are against divorce argue that it is the easy way out of difficulties and that people should make a greater effort to heal the problems in their marriages, especially if they have children. Those who support divorce see it as a compassionate law that frees people from the need to stay forever in a loveless relationship.

Christian teaching on divorce

The Bible is not clear on the subject of divorce and the Christian Church is divided on the matter. The problem is that, in the Bible, Jesus appears to give two different teachings on divorce.

In Mark, Jesus appears to forbid divorce: 'Anyone who divorces his wife and marries another woman commits adultery against her' (Mark 10:11). However, in Matthew, Jesus appears to allow for divorce in the case of unfaithfulness: 'Anyone who divorces his wife, except for marital unfaithfulness, and marries another woman commits adultery' (Matthew 19:9).

This has left many Christians confused. Is it God's will that marriage should be forever? Or should a loveless relationship be allowed to end, so that the couple can find other people to love?

The Roman Catholic Church does not allow Catholics to divorce because, it claims, Jesus banned divorce, and the marriage vows are an agreement made with God that should not be broken. Therefore, it claims, a couple can never be divorced according to God's law. A Catholic who does divorce cannot remarry in a Catholic Church.

> Between the baptised, a ratified and consummated marriage cannot be dissolved by any human power or for any reason other than death.
>
> (Catechism of the Catholic Church)

The Catholic Church allows a couple to annul their marriage in certain situations. This means the marriage never really took place. This is possible only if it can be proved that the couple did not really understand what they were doing, if they were forced into the marriage, if the marriage was not consummated (sexual intercourse did not take place), or if one of the partners was not baptised. An annulment can only be granted with the approval of a Catholic marriage tribunal.

In the Protestant Church, divorce is more readily accepted. The view is taken that humans can make mistakes and relationships do break down. Protestants believe God is always ready to forgive their sins. After asking God's forgiveness, therefore, believers may seek a divorce and are free to have another chance to find happiness with a different marriage partner. Divorced people are allowed to remarry in a Protestant Church, but those wishing to do so may be asked to talk to the minister about why their first marriage failed and to show why they believe the new marriage will last.

> Marriage should always be undertaken as a lifelong commitment but there are circumstances in which a divorced person may be married in church.
>
> (Church of England statement on marriage)

Islamic teaching on divorce

Within Islam, strict conditions are imposed on divorce, and, although permitted, it is not encouraged. Divorce is granted automatically if one partner leaves the faith, but for any other reasons the husband must announce three times over a period of 3 months his intention to divorce his wife. During this time, the husband and wife continue to live together but do not have sexual intercourse to avoid pregnancy. The couple and their families also have an opportunity to seek reconciliation. Once this period is over, they are free to remarry, although the husband is still financially responsible for his ex-wife and their children unless she remarries. In the UK, couples also need to go through a legal divorce procedure.

Islamic teachings on divorce are intended to discourage hostility, and to reduce unhappiness and hardship. A divorce should not be given in exchange for money, and the waiting period — the iddah — is very important. If the wife were pregnant, the iddah would last for the duration of her pregnancy and it would be wrong for another man to even propose to her during the iddah.

The Qur'an includes strict teaching on this:

> O Prophet, when ye do divorce women, divorce them at their prescribed periods…and fear Allah your Lord; and turn them not out of the house, nor shall they leave themselves except in case they are guilty of some open lewdness.
>
> (Surah 65:1)

The family

Christians believe children should be brought up in a loving and supportive family environment, and the importance of having children and raising a family is emphasised in the marriage service.

Nowadays there are several family types:

- **Nuclear family**: two parents and their children all living together.
- **Extended family**: parents, children and other relations such as grandparents, aunts, uncles and cousins all living close together.
- **Single-parent family**: one parent living alone with his or her children; this may be due to divorce, separation, the death of the spouse or because the parent is unmarried.
- **Reconstituted family**: where a man and woman, who have children by a previous relationship, get married and the two families become one.

Key words

Extended family
Parents, children and perhaps other relations such as grandparents, aunts, uncles and cousins all living together or close enough to see each other regularly

Nuclear family
Two parents and their children all living together

Reconstituted family
Where a man and woman, who have children by a previous relationship, get married and the two families become one

Single-parent family
One parent living alone with their children; this may be due to divorce, separation, the death of the spouse or because the parent is unmarried

Christian teaching on the family

Christians believe children are a gift from God and parents should look after them properly. The family is the setting in which children learn how to live, how to accept authority and how to learn about God. At the time of their child's baptism, Christian parents make promises to protect their child and to bring him or her up in a loving way. In return, children are expected to respect their parents' authority and, in some cases, care for them in their own times of need: 'Honour your father and your mother' (Exodus 20:12). The Bible highlights the importance of family relationships: 'Children, obey your parents.... Parents, do not exasperate your children; instead, bring them up in the instruction of the Lord' (Ephesians 6:1,4).

Christians believe all children have the right to be brought up in a loving family setting. Many Christians help charities involved with family life, including The Children's Society and NCH (formerly National Children's Home).

> The family is the community in which, from childhood, one can learn moral values, begin to honour God and make good use of freedom.
>
> (Catechism of the Catholic Church)

Churches try to help parents raise their children in a stable, Christian environment. This puts less pressure on the family unit and helps families to stay together and the marriage to be a happy one. It begins at the start of life, when the baby is brought to church for baptism. During this ceremony, parents dedicate their child to God and promise to bring him or her up in a loving Christian home. When they are older, children can make these baptismal vows for themselves in a believer's baptism or confirmation. As they grow up, children may attend Sunday school and youth groups, where young people can learn about God. There are also church schools that educate children in a Christian environment.

Churches hold family services on Sundays and special services at Christmas, Easter and harvest festival. They may also help in the running of such organisations as the Scouts and the Brownies. Many churches have a time in the weekly service that is aimed at children and in which they may participate.

Christian Churches offer help and advice to families through counselling and running organisations like the Catholic Marriage Advisory Council and the Child Welfare Council. They may also help Christian adults to look after their elderly parents through such organisations as Methodist Homes for the Aged.

Grown children have responsibilities towards their parents. As much as they can, they must give them moral support in old age and in times of illness, loneliness or distress.

(Catechism of the Catholic Church)

Islamic teaching on the family

Sharing food together is an important part of family fellowship

Key word

Zakah
Committing 2.5% of income and savings for the relief of suffering in the Muslim community

Within Islam, it is expected that there are plenty of opportunities for religious participation at home as well as at the mosque. The mother is seen to be at the heart of the Muslim family, praying for their wellbeing and taking responsibility for the religious upbringing of her children. The beliefs and values of Islam, including the principles of haram and halal, are learned first in the family. However, teaching also takes place at the madrasah, where Muslim children learn to read the Qur'an in Arabic. Some Muslim parents choose to send their children to Muslim schools, and it is an increasingly important issue whether Muslim girls, for example, should be allowed to cover in school. Going to a religious school reduces this problem as it is an accepted part of daily life. Within the mosque, too, the imam may offer advice on all matters of marriage and family life, and financial aid may be given from the **Zakah** fund in times of need.

No father can give his child anything better than good manners.

(Hadith al'Tirmidhi)

Be careful of your duty to Allah and be fair and just to your children.

(Hadith al'Bukhari)

Homosexuality

Homosexuality is sexual attraction to members of one's own sex, as opposed to **heterosexuality**, which is an attraction to members of the opposite sex. In the UK, the age of consent for homosexuality is 16. In the past, homosexuals were unable to be open about their sexual preference and the law did not recognise their relationships in a legal sense. Today, although homosexuals still cannot marry, the law does recognise the rights of partners in homosexual relationships when it comes to property and **possessions**, and homosexual partnerships can now be registered legally.

Key words

Heterosexuality
Sexual attraction to members of the opposite sex

Homosexuality
Sexual attraction to members of the same sex

Possessions
Material things which people possess or own

Christian teaching on homosexuality

Homosexual Christians face a serious problem. They wish to express their love for a partner, but feel that they are not permitted to do so because some biblical teaching appears not to support homosexual practices. However, some churches are prepared to give a blessing service to long-term homosexual relationships.

> Do not lie with a man as one lies with a woman; that is detestable.
>
> (Leviticus 18:22)

The Catholic Church is against same-sex relationships and recommends that homosexuals should stay celibate, supporting them through times of loneliness. The Catholic Church does not permit homosexuals to become priests.

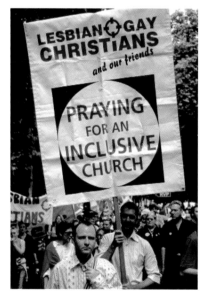

Homosexual Christians working to encourage their full acceptance into the Christian community

> Neither the sexually immoral…nor homosexual offenders will inherit the Kingdom of God.
>
> (1 Corinthians 6:9–10)

In the Church of England and other Protestant Churches, the approach towards homosexuals is more sympathetic and there is a strong gay Christian movement. Homosexual relationships are judged on the strength of the love and commitment of the partners.

There are circumstances in which individuals may justifiably choose to enter into a homosexual relationship with the hope of enjoying companionship and a physical expression of love similar to that found in marriage.

(Church of England statement on sexuality)

In the Church of England, homosexuals may become priests, but they are required to remain celibate. Many congregations will not accept a homosexual priest in their church, although this is a position that may gradually change, as the acceptance of women priests has changed. At present, however, it is still a matter that causes great division in the Church of England.

Homosexuality and the Anglican Church

Towards the end of 2004, the Archbishop of Canterbury, Dr Rowan Williams, spoke out against the dangers of homophobia which had led to the death of a young, homosexual man. The man was murdered on the South Bank in London. Dr Williams emphasised that homophobic attitudes or behaviour which could lead to murder or suicide could never be justified.

At the same time, it was revealed that Dr Williams was to chair a meeting in January 2005 of 50 Church of England bishops to discuss the way forward concerning attitudes and rulings governing homosexuality in the Anglican Church. The Lesbian and Gay Christian Movement claimed that it expected the number of same sex blessing services carried out by Anglican clergy to rise to 1,000 a year once the government's new civil partnerships law came into effect in autumn 2005. Unity among Anglican bishops on such a controversial area was thought to be vital.

The meeting was to debate the Windsor Report, which was produced in October 2004 to give guidance on the crisis in the Anglican Church concerning the homosexuality issue. Dr Williams was expected to face greatest opposition from Anglican Evangelicals who had published their own report expressing concern about the Church's attitude to same sex relationships which, they felt, directly contradicted Bible teaching.

Islamic teaching on homosexuality

Within Islam, homosexuality is seen as a grave sin and, under Shari'ah law, it is punishable by death. Al-Fatiha — a Muslim homosexual rights group — estimates that more than 4,000 homosexuals have been executed in Iran since 1979, while ten public executions of homosexuals have been performed by the Taliban army in Afghanistan.

> What! Of all creatures do ye come unto the males, and leave the wives your Lord created for you? Nay, but ye are forward folk.
>
> (Surah 26:165–66)

However, some modern Muslims are concerned to offer support to homosexual Muslims, rather than leaving them to face exclusion from the community. The website www.queerjihad.org offers help and advice for homosexual Muslims.

Questions and activities

Sample questions and answers

1 What is cohabitation? (2 marks)

Cohabitation is where a man and a woman live together without being married.

2 Outline the different Christian attitudes concerning marriage and divorce. (6 marks)

Christians believe marriage is a union of a man and a woman that is ordained by God. In Genesis 2:24, it says: 'A man will leave his father and mother and be united to his wife, and they will become one flesh.' The reason for a Christian marriage is for the couple to live together in a loving relationship in which they will respect and care for each other. It is also the setting for having lawful sex and a secure environment for having children and raising them as a Christian family. Christians believe that, ideally, marriage should be forever.

In the Roman Catholic Church, divorce is forbidden. This is because the Church believes Jesus forbade divorce: 'Anyone who divorces his wife and marries another woman commits adultery against her' (Mark 10:11). It argues that the couple made a vow before God that they would stay together forever. A divorced Catholic cannot remarry in a Catholic Church. In the Protestant Church, although divorce is not encouraged, it is accepted when the marriage relationship is clearly over and to stay together would cause the couple serious hardship or misery. Supporters of the view argue that Jesus himself suggested that divorce was permissible in certain circumstances:

'Anyone who divorces his wife, except for marital unfaithfulness, and marries another woman commits adultery' (Matthew 19:9).

A divorced person can be remarried in the Protestant Church. The view taken here is that humans make mistakes and that, if the couple seek God's forgiveness, they ought to be free to be happy with a new partner.

3 Explain why family life is important for Christians.   (8 marks)

Family life is important to Christians because the Bible teaches that children should be brought up in a loving family environment, where they can learn how to behave, care for others and love God. For Christians, marriage is the secure environment in which children should be raised and the family setting is the best way to do this. In a loving family, children can be educated, protected, nurtured and brought up to have a sense of moral value, caring for one another and loving God. The Bible says: 'Children, obey your parents in the Lord, for this is right' (Ephesians 6:1).

Many Christian couples believe children are a gift from God and that it is their duty to raise them in the Christian faith. The family unit is important to them because it gives their family a sense of belonging to a wider religious community. The Christian community represents one large family, of which each individual family is an important part.

Christians also believe the family unit is the right place to care for elderly parents. In raising children and looking after the elderly, Christians can receive a great deal of support from their Church and through such agencies as The Children's Society and Methodist Homes for the Aged.

4 'It is better to get married than to live together.' Do you agree? Give reasons for your opinion, showing you have considered another point of view. In your answer, you should refer to at least one religion.   (4 marks)

Marriage is a great commitment and, some would argue, therefore the perfect demonstration of love — that someone is prepared to make vows to another, promising to stay with them, love them and care for them for the rest of their lives. Marriage is also said to be the best environment for raising children, since their parents are committed to each other and are not just going to walk away. Marriage is a legal relationship as well and this gives the man and the woman legal rights.

For Christians, marriage is the way that God wishes men and women to be together and children to be raised.

People choose to live together (cohabit) for many reasons. Some see the time as a trial marriage, when they discover whether they really love their partner and if they can live with them forever. Others believe marriage is too much of a commitment or simply old-fashioned.

My view is that is it better for people to live together before getting married, because it is the best way to help couples decide if they really love each other enough to stay together forever. If they do not think they do, they can end the relationship without the need for a complicated divorce. However, I understand that, if the couple have children, being married might be a better option because the couple are more likely to stay together and to make an extra effort when times are hard.

Further questions

1 What is a reconstituted family? (2 marks)

2 What is promiscuity? (2 marks)

3 Outline the Christian view of homosexuality. (6 marks)

4 Explain the views of Christianity concerning sexual relationships. (8 marks)

5 'Divorce is the easy way out and should never be permitted.' Do you agree? Give reasons for your opinion, showing you have considered another point of view. (4 marks)

6 'Using contraception is against the will of God.' Do you agree? Give reasons for your opinion, showing you have considered another point of view. In your answer you should refer to one religion. (4 marks)

Class activities and homework

Understanding the importance of family life

Your teacher will divide your class into four groups. Two groups should discuss the importance of the family and the pressures that families are under today. The other two groups should look at how family life has changed over the last 50 years and consider what help the Churches might give to support families today. Under your teacher's guidance, report back to the rest of the class.

Ask some adults (for example, your parents and grandparents) how attitudes towards marriage and family life have changed since the days when they were children.

Understanding different attitudes towards sexual relationships

In pairs, divide a large sheet of paper into two columns. Write 'Pre-marital sex' in one column and 'Contraception' in the other column. List three reasons for and against each topic. Each pair should then report back to the rest of the class, which can discuss which of their reasons are the most and the least convincing. At the end, have a short class discussion and vote on which reasons were the best.

'The use of contraception is always wrong.' Do you agree? Give reasons for your opinion, showing you have considered another point of view.

Understanding divorce

Your teacher will divide your class into four groups. Each group will be given one of the following questions to answer:

- What are the arguments in favour of easy divorce?
- What are the arguments against divorce?
- What does the Bible teach about divorce?
- What are the main causes of divorce?

Each group should discuss their question, making notes as necessary. Each group should then report back to the whole class. As a class, discuss the matter of whether or not divorce should be allowed and whether it should be easier or harder to obtain than it currently is.

Do you think couples who marry in church have more or less chance of their marriage ending in divorce than couples who marry in a registry office? Explain your answer.

Understanding homosexuality

Your teacher will show you a clip from either a news or documentary programme on homosexuality (for example, homosexual priests) or from the film, *Priest* (see page 108). After watching the clip, write down at least three problems faced by homosexuals and suggest ways in which these problems may be resolved. As a class, brainstorm the answers and consider the question: 'Can the law on homosexuality be improved?'

How have attitudes towards homosexuality changed over the years?

Social harmony

Sexism

Sexism occurs when people are judged less favourably on the grounds of their sex, rather than on what they are like as people. Equality means treating people in the same way regardless of their sex, or anything else that may set them apart such as race, education, disability, sexual orientation (i.e. heterosexuality or homosexuality) or social class.

Key word

Sexism
Judging a person less favourably on the grounds of their sex

Issues of sexism are usually associated with unfavourable treatment of women, although they also include sexist treatment of men. While women in the UK have for many years had the right to own property and earn money, they have not always enjoyed the same rights as men in education, employment, inheritance or social opportunities. Until relatively recently, it was thought that women should stay at home and look after the children and not be employed outside the home. In 1900, only 15% of married women worked outside the home and many employers would not employ a married woman even if she wanted to work, on the basis that it took a job away from a man. After the two world wars, attitudes began to change. Women had to do the work of men who had gone to fight the wars, and after the fighting ended they were reluctant to give up these jobs. Times had changed and women's organisations which campaigned for equal rights became increasingly influential. Important landmarks were passed:

The suffragettes campaigned for women to have the right to vote

- The Representation of the People Act (1918) gave women aged 31 and over the right to vote.
- The Electoral Reform Act (1928) gave women aged 21 and over the right to vote and to stand as MPs.
- The Equal Pay Act (1970) gave women equal pay with men in similar jobs.
- The Sex Discrimination Act (1975) made it illegal to discriminate in jobs on the grounds of sex.

Although equality of education and employment are taken virtually for granted now, many women still feel they have to work twice as hard as men to achieve the same position. Rates of pay for men and women are still not equal and some women argue that true equality will not be achieved until people's attitudes change. However, others feel that women clearly have the same rights and opportunities as men, even if everyone does not welcome them. Attitudes to equality of the sexes are coloured by the culture in which people live, which is, in turn, invariably influenced by religious beliefs.

The Christian viewpoint

As there are many misunderstandings about the status of women within religion, it is important not to fall into the trap of making inaccurate comments such as: 'The Bible treats women as second-class citizens' or 'Muslim women are forced to cover themselves up'.

Over the last 20 years, some biblical scholars have developed new ways of interpreting the Bible. They argue that the Bible comes from a time when masculine themes and ideas dominated, and, therefore, it does not offer anything meaningful to women. New ways of interpreting the Bible have emerged, which, they claim, do greater justice to women. Genesis 2 and 3 (creation and the fall), for example, should not be interpreted as a story that approves of the oppression of women on the grounds that they ate first from the forbidden tree. The story should be read as a narrative about equality and difference between the sexes, in which both man and woman share in sin and punishment, but also share equally in God's love and grace.

Nevertheless, the Bible seems to offer differing, and sometimes conflicting, viewpoints concerning women. In some passages, the New Testament teaches that men and women are equal:

> God created man in his own image...male and female, he created them.   (Genesis 1:27)
> There is neither Jew nor Greek, slave nor free, male nor female, for you are all one in Christ.   (Galatians 3:28)

In others, men seem to be given a more dominant role:

> Wives, submit to your husbands as to the Lord. For the husband is the head of the wife as Christ is the head of the Church.
>   (Ephesians 5:22).
> Women should remain silent in churches. They are not allowed to speak, but must be in submission, as the Law says.
>   (1 Corinthians 14:34).

Jesus treated female disciples, such as Mary Magdalene, warmly

During Jesus's ministry, female disciples are treated warmly and are often presented as being far quicker to understand the identity and importance of Jesus than his male disciples. While it was male disciples (Peter and Judas) who let Jesus down in the last hours of his life, his female disciples stayed by the cross and were the first to see him after his resurrection.

The Church has tended to adopt a more equal approach to the roles of men and women in the Church and in society, and marriage is seen as uniting equals under God: 'May her husband put his trust in her and recognise that she is his equal and the heir with him to the life of grace' (Catholic wedding service).

One of the most important changes came in 1994 when the Church of England allowed women to become priests (to be ordained). However, the Catholic Church does not admit women to ordination. Opposition to the ordination of women is based on several arguments, mainly those of St Paul, who wrote: 'A woman should learn in quietness and submission. I do not permit a woman to teach or to have authority over a man: she must be silent' (1 Timothy 2:11). The fact that Jesus did not include women in his inner circle of 12 disciples is also used by those who oppose the ordination of women: 'The Lord Jesus chose men to form the twelve apostles and the apostles did the same when they chose their successors.... For this reason the ordination of women is not possible' (Catechism of the Catholic Church).

Women and men work together in many forms of Christian ministry

These reasons are now thought to be out of date by many Christians. Christians who are in favour of women priests and ordained ministers often highlight the different skills they can offer to their congregations. Women may be in a particularly strong position to offer loving and sympathetic care to those in need, especially women and young people who are suffering. Moreover, some Christians may prefer to work with a female minister, so the needs of the congregation are better met by having both men and women in leadership in the Church.

Nevertheless, for some, the ordination of women is still a difficult issue. Many Christians, including some women, left the Church of England after women were admitted to the priesthood.

Women in Islam

Islam believes men and women are equal in matters of religion and education, and that every instruction given in the Qur'an applies equally to male and female Muslims:

For Muslim men and women, for believing men and women, for devout men and women, for true men and women, for men and women who are patient and constant, for men and women who humble themselves, for men and women who give in charity, for men and women who fast, for men and women who guard their chastity, and for men and women who engage much in Allah's praise, for them has Allah prepared forgiveness and great reward.

(Surah 33:35)

Islam regards men and women as being of the same essence created from a single soul:

O mankind! Reverence your Guardian-Lord, who created you from a single person, created of like nature, his mate, and from this pair scattered (like seeds) countless men and women. Reverence Allah, through whom you demand your mutual (rights), and reverence the wombs (that bore you); for Allah ever watches over you.

(Surah 4:1)

As a result, men and women share the same rights and responsibilities, and neither is superior to the other.

Muslim women have a crucial role to play in the home, bringing up children in the knowledge of Islam and following the rules of halal housekeeping. Women are separated from men in the mosque. While they are free to work, women can expect to be provided for by their husbands. For this reason, men are given 'a degree of advantage' over women (Surah 2:228) because they ultimately bear the responsibility for providing for the family. Therefore, women can only inherit half as much as men, and the husband has the right to begin divorce proceedings.

Muslim girls wearing hijab

In some Muslim cultures, women are expected to wear a chador when outside the home. This is a full-length cloak, designed so that women cannot be identified by strangers. The purpose of these coverings, often worn with a veil or hijab to cover the face, is to give women freedom from men looking at them, the root word 'hajaba' meaning to hide from view or conceal. Although the Qur'an does not insist on women being fully veiled, it is recommended and supported by the Hadiths.

> As regards the veiling of women, I said 'O Allah's Apostle! I wish you ordered your wives to cover themselves from the men because good and bad ones talk to them.'
>
> (Hadith)

> O Prophet! Tell thy wives and thy daughters and the women of the believers to draw their cloaks close around them. That will be better, so that they may be recognised and not annoyed. Allah is ever forgiving, merciful.
>
> (Surah 33:59)

Some Muslims argue that this practice is outdated; others suggest that any identification of religious belief in public should be discouraged in order to maintain an equal society. However, many women who wear the chador seem to feel that it gives them a mark of protection, allowing them to maintain a certain privacy in public. It also identifies that the woman is committed to her faith.

Racism

Racism is the belief that certain ethnic groups are superior to others. **Racial prejudice** has led to many injustices, including the slave trade and official policies of segregation in several US states between the 1880s and 1960s. In 1866, reconstruction after the civil war prevented the restriction of

Key word

Racial prejudice
The view that certain races are inferior or superior

the rights of black people, but this movement angered many white suprema-cists. Groups such as the Ku Klux Klan waged an illegal war on black people. Thousands were killed in the Deep South by such organisations and in 1877 reconstruction was ended. Segregation was sanctioned by the so-called 'Jim Crow' laws. This name originated from a song performed by the entertainer Daddy Rice, who sang with his face covered in charcoal in a stereotypical image of a black man. In many areas, black and white citizens were separated on buses, trains, restaurants and other public places. There were separate schools for blacks and whites and intermarriage was prohibited in some states, including Arizona and Florida.

The annual Notting Hill carnival in London demonstrates Britain's multi-ethnic and multi-racial society

Key words

Multi-ethnic
A society that consists of people from different cultural backgrounds

Multi-racial
A society that consists of people from different racial backgrounds

Racial discrimination
Treating people less favourably, and considering them to be less worthy, on the grounds of their race

Racial harmony
A society in which people of different races live together in peace

Tokenism
Including one or two members of racial minorities to ensure that no claim can be made of racism

By contrast, the UK seems to have become a racially mixed society more easily. It has welcomed and offered asylum to those suffering persecution abroad, such as Jews during the Second World War. After the British empire came to an end, the UK government allowed massive immigration from Commonwealth countries and many people came to Britain from different racial and ethnic (belief and culture) groups. As a result, Britain is a **multi-ethnic** and **multi-racial** society.

This has not been achieved without difficulties, however, and in the 1950s and 1960s many people feared immigrants from the Commonwealth would take white people's houses and jobs. Consequently, many immigrants had to settle for the poorest-paid jobs and had to live in the poorest areas. This is an example of **racial discrimination**, by which people are treated less favourably because of their racial or ethnic origin. This is in direct contrast to **racial harmony**, when different races live together in peace.

The Race Relations Act 1976 made it unlawful to discriminate against anyone because of race, colour, ethnic or national origin, whether in terms of employment, housing, education or welfare services. It was also made illegal to stir up racial hated, whether it be in speeches or in print. The UK government set up the Commission for Racial Equality to fight racism and to educate the public about the importance of racial equality. Nevertheless, claims are still made that many institutions are racist.

In response, some employers and organisations make a point of employing a few non-white people in order to appear to be encouraging racial equality. This is called **tokenism** and can cause as many problems as racism.

Religion and racism

Any form of racism is strictly prohibited in both Christianity and Islam. According to the teachings of both, all people are equal.

Christianity

In Christianity, God is the only true judge of people: 'The spiritual man makes judgements about all things, but he himself is not subject to any man's judgement' (1 Corinthians 2:15). It is also believed that all people are made in God's image and are equally valuable to God:

> God does not show favouritism, but accepts men from every nation.
>
> (Acts 10:34–35)

> There is neither Jew nor Greek...you are all one in Christ.
>
> (Galatians 3:28)

Jesus himself treated members of different races equally: he healed a Roman's servant (Luke 7:1–10); he talked intimately with a Samaritan woman (John 4:7–26); and the parable of the good Samaritan shows that races which hated each other should follow God's command to 'Love your neighbour as yourself' (Luke 10:27).

Within the Church of England, the Race and Community Relations Committee acts as a watchdog over issues of racism and problems of unemployment and imprisonment among black people. The Committee on Black Anglican Concerns helps Churches to develop anti-racist opportunities for black people to play an active role.

> We affirm that racism is a direct contradiction of the gospel of Jesus.
>
> (Methodist Church)

> Every form of social and cultural discrimination must be curbed and eradicated as incompatible with God's design.
>
> (Catechism of the Catholic Church)

Muslims on Hajj surround the Ka'ba

Islam

Islam has no barriers based on race:

> O mankind! We created you from a single pair of a male and female, and made you into nations and tribes that ye may know each other. Verily the most honoured of you in the sight of Allah is the most righteous of you.
>
> (Surah 49:13)

Within Islam, all Muslims are part of the ummah — the worldwide community of Muslims of all races and colours, united by their faith. Unity among Muslims is emphasised by praying in Arabic, and facing the qiblah (direction) of Makkah during prayer. The Hajj unites Muslims from all over the world, and the month of Ramadan unites them globally at times of fasting and feasting. The revelation of the Qur'an was intended for all races — 'O humanity, I am the messenger of God to you all!' (Surah 7:158) — so no one race can claim superiority over another. In 2003 Ruquaiyyah Waris

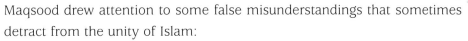

Maqsood drew attention to some false misunderstandings that sometimes detract from the unity of Islam:

- Muslims are not all Arab or Pakistani; there is no chosen race and all races are loved by God.
- Muslim is not to be equated with 'brown skin', since many people with brown skin are non-Muslim, and many Muslims are not brown skinned.
- Muslims are not uneducated or backward, or from countries that are undeveloped.
- Muslims do not usually fit the stereotypes presented by the media.

Religious pluralism

The UK is a **multi-faith** society that practises **religious pluralism** — an acceptance of all faiths as having an equal right to co-exist. Its citizens have **religious freedom**, which means members of all religions are free to worship and have equal political rights. There are about 30 million people who claim to be Christian in the UK, with about 1 million Muslims and 300,000 Jews and Hindus respectively. However, it should be remembered that many people in the UK claim to be Christian on the basis of tradition rather than belief, so this figure does not accurately represent those who have an active Christian faith.

As a multi-faith nation, the UK has a varied and rich cultural life which represents different viewpoints, cultures and beliefs. Although this is seen by many as an exciting way to live, some Christians express concern about the effect that religious pluralism has on Christianity. If, as some Christians believe, Christianity is the only way to come into a relationship with God, the prominence of other religions in the UK may encourage more people to see all religions as an equally valid route to God. The view that only one religion can be true is called **exclusivism**. This view can be worrying, especially if some Christians claim that non-Christians are destined for hell. As a result, some Christians believe it is

Key words

Exclusivism
The view that only those who belong to one particular faith can be saved from condemnation

Multi-faith
A society that consists of people from different faiths

Religious freedom
Members of all religions are free to worship and have equal political rights

Religious pluralism
An acceptance of all faiths as having equal rights to co-exist

their duty to try to convert everyone to Christianity — a view not shared by members of other religions.

> The Church still has the obligation and also the sacred right to evangelise all men.
>
> (Catechism of the Catholic Church)

> Jesus said, 'I am the way and the truth and the life. No one comes to the father except through me.'
>
> (John 14:6)

Key words

Inclusivism
The view that all religions have some truth and should be able to teach and practise without restriction or prejudice

In contrast, **inclusivism** allows that, while Christianity has the whole truth, other religions have part of the truth and should be allowed to continue their search for God unhindered.

> The Catholic Church recognises in other religions the search for the God who is unknown yet near.
>
> (Catechism of the Catholic Church)

Many Churches and religious groups, including the Council of Christians and Jews and the Inter-faith Network for the United Kingdom, have been working together to heal divisions between different faiths. Such groups represent a wide range of religious beliefs and seek to increase understanding and awareness based on the view that God created all humanity to have a relationship with him, and sent Jesus to unite, not divide, them. Some religious thinkers go so far as to say that all who believe in God should be united in a single fellowship, in which terms such as 'Christian' and 'Muslim' are no longer used.

Relationships with other religions

Martin Luther King Jr

Martin Luther King Jr was born in Atlanta on 15 January 1929 to a middle-class black family. His father, Martin Luther King Sr, was a minister at Ebenezer Baptist Church and a strong-willed man with a powerful influence on his son. On one occasion, King and his father were in Atlanta and were told by a sales assistant to move to the 'appropriate' area in the store before they could be served. King Sr said that he would either buy the shoes from where he and his son already were or they would leave. They left. Martin recalls that after this incident, he said: 'I don't care how long I have to live with this system, I'll never accept it.'

King was educated in local grammar and high schools and in 1944 attended Morehouse College in Atlanta. He was a direct contradiction to the stereo-typical black person as seen by many whites. King was hard working and achieved a PhD in his mid-twenties. He studied the work and philosophy of Gandhi and came to believe that violence only brought about more violence and hatred. King made a trip to India in 1959, where he came into contact with many of Gandhi's followers — thereafter he was inspired by them. Jesus condemned violence and this was apparent on more than one occasion. When he was arrested, one of his disciples cut off the ear of one of the guards arresting him. Jesus rebuked him, saying: 'Those who live by the sword die by the sword' (Matthew 26:52). More famously, he said: 'If your enemy slaps you on your right cheek, turn and offer him your left' (Matthew 5:39).

After the trip to India, King became the pastor of Dexter Avenue Baptist Church. He faced criticism for the first time when he became a member of both the National Association for the Advancement of Colored People (NAACP) and the Alabama Council on Human Relations. He was accused of having dual loyalties to two organisations with very different approaches to the problem. His response was: 'This question betrays the assumption that there is only one solution to the race problem.' He continued his relationship with both organisations and refused the presidency of the NAACP in 1955.

In the same year, a 15-year-old girl denied her seat to a white man on a bus. She was removed from the bus and arrested. King was a member of a committee formed by the black community to protest to the proper authorities. The committee met with the manager of the Montgomery bus company and the police commissioner. Both apologised and promised to change things. They admitted that the driver was wrong and that action would be taken against him. They also said that a definite policy on bus seating would be issued. Neither of these promises were kept and the girl was convicted and given a suspended sentence. Soon after, a famous incident involving Rosa Parks brought up the issue again. She too refused to give up her seat for a white man on a bus and was arrested. Calls for a bus boycott were issued. King told a story of a black maid who found one of the leaflets, which she was unable to read herself. She asked her mistress to tell her what the leaflet was about, but her mistress immediately told the local newspaper of what 'the uppity niggers are doing'. Ironically, this helped the boycott to flourish. More of the black community heard about it and took part. King watched the empty buses drive past his house, and was assured that the boycott had been successful.

King's non-violent tactics were put to the ultimate test in 1963 during a mass protest. The fact that the police dealt with the marchers brutally gave everyone a real idea of the degree of racism across the nation. King was arrested, but this did not stop him. Later that year he was a principal speaker at the march on Washington where he delivered his most famous speech:

> I have a dream that my four little children will one day live in a nation where they will not be judged by the color of their skin but by the content of their character...

> The sweltering summer of the colored people's legitimate discontent will not pass until there is an invigorating autumn of freedom and equality.

He was awarded the 1964 Nobel peace prize.

On his return from Washington, King brought his crusade to Chicago, where he was responsible for launching programmes to improve the slums and provide housing. Angry young black people, who paid little notice to his teachings, came to his attention. They were not at all interested in his pleas for non-violent protest and their attitude was a major motivation to King as he took an interest in the war in Vietnam. The war had pointed him to a prominent issue: poverty. By threatening national boycotts and protests, King pressed for a guaranteed family income. He began to plan a massive march of the poor on Washington DC, which would leave Congress with no choice but to recognise the huge number of desperately poor Americans.

King's plans were disrupted when he was sidetracked by trying to discourage violence while supporting the Memphis sanitation men's strike. Tragically, he was never able to return to his poverty ideals. On 4 April 1968, while standing on the balcony of the Lorraine Hotel off Beale Street alongside Jesse Jackson and Ralph Abernathy, King was shot in the neck. Ironically, there was a sudden wave of violence across the country as a result of his assassination — precisely what he would not have wanted.

Malcolm X

Malcolm X was born Malcolm Little on 19 May 1925 in Nebraska, to a family of eight children. His father, Earl Little, was a Baptist minister and a supporter of the Black Nationalist leader Marcus Garvey. His civil rights activities led to death threats from white supremacist groups such as the Black Legion. In 1929, the family's Michigan house was burned to the ground, and 2 years later Earl's mutilated body was found on the town's trolley tracks. The Littles and many of the black community suspected this to be the work of the Ku Klux Klan. The family endured a hard life of poverty after Earl's death, and Malcolm's mother was eventually committed to a mental institution.

Malcolm was elected class president at Mason Junior High School, was interested in English and history, played basketball for the team and graduated at the top of his class. It was his dream to become a lawyer, but this was crushed after a favourite teacher of his told him: 'That is not a realistic goal for a nigger. You need to start thinking about something you can be'. It was suggested he try carpentry instead. Malcolm's behaviour changed drastically after this and he lost touch with his white acquaintances, feeling he would never succeed in a white society.

As an adult, Malcolm X became known as 'Big Red'. He became involved in drugs, prostitution and petty crime and ultimately spent much of his life in prison. During a 7-year prison sentence for burglary, his brother Reginald told him of a religious organisation, the Nation of Islam. Malcolm studied its teachings and learnt about the leader, Elijah Muhammad. Muhammad taught that white society tried to keep black people from helping themselves and achieving success in many areas. The Nation of Islam was fighting for a separate state of its own with only black citizens. After he was freed, Malcolm became a devoted follower and took the surname 'X'. Later, as a minister and spokesman for the Nation of Islam, he spread its message through television shows and radio programmes, and was credited for increasing its membership numbers from 500 in 1952 to 30,000 in 1963.

According to Malcolm, it was Hajj that transformed him against racism:

> There were tens of thousands of pilgrims from all over the world.... But we were all participating in the same ritual, displaying a spirit of unity and brotherhood that my experiences in America had led me to believe could not exist between the white and non-white.
>
> (Quoted in Louis Lomax, *To Kill a Black Man*, 1968)

His change in outlook led him to start preaching not only to black people but to all races: 'I believe in treating people right, but I'm not going to waste my time trying to treat somebody right who doesn't know how to return the treatment.' However, Malcolm X was not convinced that the only way to fight for freedom was non-violently: 'We are non-violent with people who are non-violent with us.' The racial tension during the 1960s was immense and the FBI kept a close watch on the Nation of Islam's activities. In 1963, Malcolm learnt that Elijah Muhammad was having relationships with several women in the Nation of Islam, some of whom had borne his children. Malcolm was deeply hurt by this deception and refused to keep the matter quiet. In turn, Malcolm was criticised for observing, after John F. Kennedy's assassination: 'Kennedy never foresaw that the chickens would come home to roost.'

Muhammad silenced him for 90 days, but Malcolm suspected that there was more to it than just the criticism of Kennedy. He terminated his relationship with the Nation of Islam in March 1964, and founded the Muslim Mosque Inc. He was willing to cooperate with local civil rights activists, but remained unable to accept the idea that the civil rights movement could be seen as a revolution: 'There can be no revolution without bloodshed and it is nonsense to describe the civil rights movement as a revolution.' When asked for his opinion on the work of Martin Luther King, Malcolm X said: 'Dr King wants the same thing I want. Freedom.' Throughout his career, Malcolm was criticised for his methods, but many of those writing about him tend to forget that his main belief was one of brotherhood. He made it clear that those who were out to harm members of other ethnic groups or races were the ones he felt did not deserve to be dealt with non-violently: 'I am not a racist. I am against every form of racism and segregation, every form of discrimination. I believe in human beings and that all human beings should be respected as such, regardless of their color.'

Malcolm was warned on several occasions that his life was in danger, but he was not deterred. In February 1965, Malcolm's family home was firebombed. Luckily, the members of his family escaped any injury. For the vast majority of his career, he was seen as a controversial figure, and his rejection of the Nation of Islam won him further enemies. While speaking at an engagement in Manhattan on 21 February 1965, Malcolm was shot by three gunmen: Talmadge Hayer, Norman Butler and Thomas Johnson were all members of the Nation of Islam. At the age of 39, Malcolm was pronounced dead at New York Colombia Presbyterian Hospital. His funeral was attended by 1,500 people.

Writing nearly 40 years after the assassinations of Martin Luther King and Malcolm X, Michael Moore claims in his book *Stupid White Men* (2002) that very little has really changed in the USA: 'I believe that we've become so used to this image of the black man as a predator that we are forever ruined by this brainwashing.' In order to hide prejudice, he claims, the people of the USA hold a black history month, recognise Martin Luther King Day and give money to the United Negro College Fund, but statistics tell a different story. About 20% of black people between the ages of 16 and 24 are not in school or working, whereas only 9% of white people of those ages are in the same situation. Black levels of unemployment have been roughly twice those of the white population since 1954. Moore makes his points light-heartedly, but claims that they are supported by statistics, stressing that even though it is said that racism is recognised as wrong, this is not demonstrated in everyday life:

> At work, the whites still get the plum job, double the pay, and a seat in the front of the bus to happiness and success. Look back down the aisle though, and you'll see the blacks sitting where they've always been, picking up after us, waiting on us, serving us from behind the counter.

Islam and other religions

Islam believes that freedom of worship for all people is to be respected, and that Islam should not be forced on anyone. Furthermore, Christians and Jews, called 'people of the book' (i.e. the Old Testament/Jewish Tenakh), are given special status in the Qur'an, and a Muslim man is free to marry a Christian or Jewish woman without obliging her to convert.

Nonetheless, Muslims believe that Islam is the one true faith, the final word of Allah given to the Prophet Muhammad, the 'Seal of the Prophets', perfect and complete. Because of this, Muslims believe they have a responsibility to convert non-Muslims to Islam.

At the moment, Islam is a growing religion in the UK, and there is an increasing number of converts from all races. At the same time, some Muslims are concerned that the effects of living in a multi-cultural, and often secular (non-religious), society are not good for British Muslims. Muslim children often face social pressures to drink alcohol, eat non-halal food, have sexual relationships before and outside marriage, and to have greater freedom outside the family unit, all of which can have a weakening effect on the Muslim community.

It may well be the task of Muslim converts to interpret Islam's spiritual message to the western world, and even to help wavering Muslims, who are succumbing to the secular society.

(Ruquaiyyah Waris Maqsood, *Teach Yourself Islam*, 1998)

Questions and activities

Sample questions and answers

1 What is meant by the term 'prejudice'? (2 marks)

Prejudice occurs when someone judges or makes a decision about someone else on the basis of his or her colour, sex, beliefs, age or other aspect.

2 Outline the attitudes of one religion other than Christianity to the role of women. (6 marks)

Islam draws on the Qur'an and the Hadiths in its teaching on the role of women. Although many people believe that the attitude of Islam towards women is constricting, this is not the intention. Women are highly regarded within Islam and are to be protected from unwanted attention and respected, not only as wives and mothers, but as persons in their own right. Although women do not have positions of religious authority in Islam, they are still part of the Ummah, and although separate from men in the mosque, they pray together and are not forbidden from studying the Qur'an.

Many Muslim women choose to adopt traditional dress which involves some degree of covering, perhaps a hijab or head covering, or fuller covering concealing the whole body. The practice of covering is intended to protect the woman and gives her greater, not lesser, respect. She is not seen as an object of desire for strangers, and she does not need to compete with other women. Many Muslim women say that they feel liberated by being covered as it enables them to concentrate on their religious, family and business lives without harassment.

Although the woman's first priority is thought to be her home and family, there is no prohibition on her earning a living, owning property or entering into legal contracts, and her husband has no claim on her earnings. In fact, the husband is still responsible for providing for her, even if she is able to be financially independent.

3 Explain why living in a multi-faith society may cause problems for a religious believer. (8 marks)

In a multi-faith society, people of many religious faiths live together. There is no particular emphasis on, or provision for, any one religion and there are places of worship for different faiths. Different religious communities celebrate their festivals and carry out practices and customs according to their beliefs. This can cause problems for religious believers who feel that not enough provision is made for their particular faith and that they are living in a society which only acknowledges their faith in a rather superficial way, and doesn't understand its real needs.

For example, in a Muslim country where everyone responds to the call to prayer, schools and employers are prepared for their pupils and employees to do so too. In a multi-faith society, although a prayer room may be provided, it is harder for Muslims to leave their work or class to pray, even though it may be tolerated.

Christians who adopt an exclusivist view and believe that Christianity is the only true faith may have problems living in a multi-faith society. They may feel uncomfortable living alongside members of other faiths if they cannot encourage them to become Christians. They may also feel that the distinctiveness of Christianity is lost in a society in which Christian festivals such as Christmas are just called holidays to avoid stressing their Christian significance in a society which tries to accommodate people of many faiths.

4 'Religion helps people to live in peace together.' Do you agree? Give reasons for your opinion, showing you have considered another point of view. (4 marks)

Religion helps people to live in peace together because if people share the same faith, they are likely to share the same attitudes towards life. They are also likely to have similar viewpoints and standards of behaviour, so there will be fewer causes of conflict. It does not, however, follow that believers do have the same viewpoints. Even within the same religion, there are those who cannot agree with each other. For example, in Christianity, there is a wide range of differing views concerning such matters as marriage and divorce. Religious believers can live in peace together and their common belief in God enables them to worship together and share with and help one another. However, this is less true in a multi-faith society, where members of different religions often clash, not only about their religions but also on matters in the wider world. Many conflicts around the world have their origins in a clash of religious ideals. In my opinion, religious believers ought to be able to live in peace together, since all religions highlight the importance of people loving one another and living in harmony. However, the reality is very different and the suffering caused by religious conflict in many countries and among many communities around the world does not encourage the ideal that religion will help everyone to live in peace.

Further questions

1 What is meant by the term 'discrimination'? (2 marks)
2 What is meant by the term 'racism'? (2 marks)
3 Outline the views of Christianity on the roles of men and women. (6 marks)
4 Explain the attitudes of one religion other than Christianity to racial equality. (8 marks)
5 'Religious believers should always marry within their community.' Do you agree? Give reasons for your opinion, showing you have considered another point of view. (4 marks)
6 'No religion genuinely practises equality between men and women.' Do you agree? Give reasons for your opinion, showing you have considered another point of view. (4 marks)

Class activities and homework

Understanding sexism

In pairs or small groups, make a list of the qualities that may be considered traditionally male or female traits. Remember that these traits can be shared by both males and females, but think about why some may be associated more with one sex rather than the other. Under your teacher's guidance, discuss the lists in class.

Read the following passages in the Bible, all of which describe incidents involving women in the ministry of Jesus: Mark 15:40–41, Luke 23:27 and John 4:7–30. What do you consider to be most interesting and significant about these accounts?

Understanding racism

Read Acts 10:1–16. This is about Peter's vision, which convinced him that God welcomed people of all races into the kingdom of heaven. This was not an easy lesson for Peter, a Jew, to accept, but it had important consequences for the growth of the early Church. Then look at the parable of the good Samaritan in Luke 10:25–37. In small groups or pairs, devise modern versions of these narratives, showing how they could be used to address issues of racism in the modern world and your community in particular. Under your teacher's guidance, share your modern versions with the rest of the class.

Look at a local newspaper regularly over a period of a couple of weeks and keep a record of examples of claims of racist behaviour or attitudes.

Understanding religious pluralism

Under your teacher's guidance, discuss what factors make members of different religions in your school or class feel more or less united and accepted by each other. Use the opportunity to ask questions about your classmates' different religious traditions and beliefs. Write down one question aimed at understanding another religion better on a small piece of paper. Your teacher will read each question aloud. Whoever in your class is able to provide an answer should do so. For example, a student could ask a Muslim classmate: 'Do you find it difficult to maintain fasting during Ramadan?'

'Religious unity is a dream, but can never be a reality. There is far too much misunderstanding.' Discuss this claim, giving your opinion but showing you have considered other points of view.

Religion and the media

The nature of the media

The term 'the media' refers to television, radio, newspapers and film — all the means of mass communication which, in the twentieth and twenty-first centuries, have been joined by the ever-increasing forces of e-communication, especially the internet. The rapid growth of media and telecommunications technology has made the media powerful in shaping people's political views and opinions on public and private behaviour. The media also reflect society's values; while it may be true to say that they influence opinion, they also respond to society's demands. Public taste and demand work hand in hand with the media, and the result is the incredible range of entertainment and information that is available to us today with barely the flick of a switch.

The influence of the media

The forms of media that this unit is concerned with are television, news-papers and film. Television plays an important role in the lives of people of all ages and statistics suggest that the average UK viewer watches television for 28 hours per week. Television plays a major role in influencing people's consumer choices — the products they buy, who they vote for, what is in and out of fashion, what music they listen to. In recent years, there has been a considerable increase in 'reality' programmes, and a growing obsession with the people who emerge with some degree of fame from these

situations. Similarly, the media are responsible for encouraging a bizarre interest in so-called 'celebrities' — individuals who, for a variety of reasons, have become figures of public interest. They are used by the media to increase readership and viewing statistics, but these 'celebrities' do not encourage people to see their own lives as valuable.

Television can influence minds from an early age

The media are closely associated with advertising — they encourage the public to buy and consume goods and services. Many of these goods and services are not essential and may drive the consumer into debt. Debt, gambling, materialism and greed are, naturally, areas that concern religious believers. Most people fall victim to the influence of the media at some time or other. Most often this influence is harmless, but when it is not, it can cause great damage to people's lives.

As a result, some religious believers have rejected mass media altogether. They may choose not to buy or watch television, only to read religious magazines or newspapers, and to exercise strict controls over what they see at the cinema or theatre. Easy access to the internet has brought further problems, and it is not just religious parents who seek to keep their children away from the more unpleasant sides of life that find their way onto the internet.

The media exist to represent every aspect of society, within reason, and to do so with as little bias as possible. However, religious believers may claim that the media often distort the truth, and are guilty of promoting worldly values — those which do not correspond with what most religious believers would consider loving and strengthening for the community and the individual. When people watch a lot of television, their critical faculties — their ability to tell right from wrong and to distinguish between good and evil — can become confused. Religious believers, leaders and institutions see that they have an important role to play in balancing things out. This may be done through offering alternative media or educating people to be careful about what they watch and read, equipping them with the skills to make balanced and truthful judgements rather than simply accepting media information at face value.

What can the media offer?

It would be unfair to paint an entirely negative picture of the media. There is no doubt that the media enable people to gain a wide knowledge of the world, government and politics, culture, literature, religion, music and art, as well as sport, science and current affairs. The media play a vital role in education as well as entertainment, and many teachers use a range of material from the media in class to offer vital support to formal teaching materials. People can also find the media useful in helping them to discover their own talents and strengths. It is clear, therefore, that, used wisely, the media can improve people's lives.

Religious broadcasting

When the BBC was established, it was taken for granted that Britain was a Christian country, and religious broadcasting was a key part of its programming. Today, Britain is a multi-cultural, multi-faith society, which many feel should be reflected in religious broadcasting. Some people object to daily radio programmes such as *Pause for Thought* and *Thought for the Day* because they think it is unfair that religious speakers should be able to speak on air without their opinions being challenged.

Broadcasting regulations in the UK forbid religious organisations to recruit members on air. While some religious broadcasts have an obvious focus towards a particular faith — for example, *Songs of Praise*, which is clearly Christian orientated — they are never evangelistic. Programmes on satellite

Father Ted: comedy is often used to deal with religion on television

television are not bound by the same restrictions, and their broadcasts often include gospel messages that are intended to encourage viewers to make a faith commitment. Within regular television programmes, comedy is often used as a device to deal with religious issues and situations — *The Vicar of Dibley* or *Father Ted*, for example. It is worth thinking about what this says about the way television writers think their audience views religious life and people.

The Broadcasting Act 1990 made religious broadcasting of some kind a legal requirement in the UK, but there is great division over what is enough and what is too much, and what the content of that broadcasting should be. In 2002, the Church of England Synod (the governing body of the Church of England) looked at religious broadcasting. It found that many people were unhappy that it had been reduced. At the same time, the National Secular Society objected that so much of Radio 4 dealt with religious topics even in programmes that were not specifically religious.

In 2000, the arts and media journal, *Cultural Trends,* carried out a study of religious broadcasting. It arrived at the following figures:

- 54% of adults saw at least one religious programme in 1 month in 1998.
- No changes had been made to the level of religious broadcasting on ITV and the BBC since 1988.
- The launch of Channel 5 increased the overall level of religious broadcasting.
- Religious broadcasting had become more varied and drew bigger audiences among viewers aged between 16 and 44 than among those aged over 45.
- The study reached the following conclusion:

> It is time that religious broadcasting was regarded as having a positive contribution to make to the health of multi-cultural Britain. This research shows that today's religious broadcasting is far removed from the popular image of ladies in hats singing hymns.

Regular religious broadcasting

Regular religious broadcasting is not just about church services. Important services, such as royal weddings or other state occasions, are broadcast and, at key times of the year, special services such as Christmas celebrations are shown. Perhaps one of the few religious services that the vast majority of the population watched was the funeral of Princess Diana in 1997, when a whole nation seemed to be touched with an uncharacteristic degree of grief and spirituality. More recently, in April 2005, the funeral of Pope John Paul II was broadcast across the world. The death of the pope was given enormous coverage in the media, perhaps revealing the level of people's interest in global religious matters, even in a largely non-religious society.

The funeral of Pope John Paul II, 2005

Songs of Praise

Although relatively few church services are broadcast, *Songs of Praise*, a long-standing part of BBC religious programming, is shown every Sunday in the early evening. It is frequently based around a church community and shows people involved in active worship in at least part of the programme. *Songs of Praise* is essentially a worship programme which uses a magazine format, featuring interviews, musical items, readings and news. It focuses on religious issues but in the style of a chat show or news and human-interest programme. The programme aims to be up to date and relevant, and so it is sometimes based around a traditional church and music, but it often includes inspirational and religious music of many kinds, even Christian rock and soul music, with solo items as well as congregational singing. *Songs of Praise* is hosted by a number of presenters, including Aled Jones and Alan Titchmarsh, who have won fame in other areas of the media. Presumably the intention is that viewers should be able to identify the presenters from their other context, and that this should make them more popular and easy to relate to.

On Sunday 31 October 2004, *Songs of Praise* hosted a special programme on the role of the Bible and the part it has played in transforming many people's lives. It was hosted by Jonathan Edwards, the former Olympic triple jumper, who has become almost as famous for being a Christian as for being an athlete. Interviews with people were interspersed with musical items, all of which were contemporary, accompanied by a typical rock band line-up of keyboard, lead and bass guitars, drums, a lead singer and a backing singer, or a soloist singing to her own guitar accompaniment. The influential Bible smuggler, Brother Andrew, who smuggled Bibles into Eastern Europe, spoke of his experiences, including the times when he needed God to keep him safe from border guards. Another brief interview was held with Richard Taylor, a former teenage drug addict, who was converted in prison after one night reading the Bible instead of tearing out a page to use to roll a cigarette. He is now an ordained minister and believes he was called by God to give something back for the incredible transformation that took place in his life.

The programme included a brief summary of the founding of the British and Foreign Bible Society, which was established after young Mary Jones had saved for 6 years and walked 25 miles to the home of Thomas Charles to buy a Bible. He was so touched by this that he founded the society in 1804 to make Bibles more widely available, and only 4 years later the society was at work in 130 countries around the world. A spokesman for the society today explained the principle of a recent advertising campaign, which encouraged the public to see the Bible as a source of answers to dilemmas raised in soap operas.

Jonathan Edwards also spoke with the actor Rob Lacey, who wrote *The Street Bible* after he had been diagnosed with cancer. It reflects his own beliefs as well as his desire to show how the Bible could be made easier for people to understand.

Jonathan
Edwards

The Heaven and Earth Show

The Heaven and Earth Show is a religious magazine programme, shown every Sunday morning on BBC1. It features guests from a range of backgrounds. Its style is informal, encouraging viewers to participate in the programme by texting, e-mailing or phoning during the show.

In a typical programme, the presenters address a headline moral or spiritual issue, which forms the basis for viewers' feedback and participation, and follow through with a range of features on ethical, spiritual and cultural issues. Some programmes include special features, such as that on belief in the UK shown on Sunday 7 September 2003. Representatives of three groups — believers, New Age followers and atheists/agnostics — were present in the studio, responding to issues raised by a specially commissioned MORI poll. The poll produced some interesting results:

- 81% of people who responded to a telephone vote said they believed in God.
- Although scientific knowledge has increased in the last 100 years, the decline in religious belief that had been expected does not seem to have taken place.
- The family is still the main channel for passing on religion, although people tend to discover spirituality through personal experience.
- There are far more spiritual options available today than in the past — those seeking a religion have a huge range of choices, including New Age religions.
- 17% of people said they were mainly influenced by the media — the same figure as were influenced by religion.
- Attendance at traditional churches appears to be declining, but attendance at Evangelical and Charismatic churches continues to rise.

The programme televised on 31 October 2004 followed the more regular format. The issue for discussion and response throughout the programme was conscience versus country: would you fight for your country if required? Two studio guests represented different perspectives, debating the question of where loyalty lies today — with self, family, country or religion? It was suggested that moral values have not changed significantly over the last 50 years, but that the reasons for holding those values have changed, with younger generations less influenced by religious authority than by social morality.

A special feature on Ramadan ran throughout the hour-long broadcast. Three Muslims — a fireman who had converted 8 years previously when he had married his Muslim wife, a 17-year-old A-level student, and a DJ on Mashal

Radio — were interviewed about the significance of Ramadan for them and how they coped with fasting during daylight hours for 30 days. All were very positive about the experience — they valued the special nature of the sacrifice they were making and were encouraged by the community spirit among Muslims that is highlighted during the festival.

The programme also included a feature on ethical clothing and fair-trade fashion, based on the fact that for every £100 spent on clothes, 40p goes to the worker who made them. In the UK, £23 billion is spent annually on clothes, and yet the cost to the environment is rarely considered. This item made a convincing case for buying second-hand clothing, but with no overtly religious message.

The religious significance was even smaller in a repeat of an interview with DJ John Peel, who had died the previous week, and a new interview with 1960s pop star, Marianne Faithful. A few brief comments were made in the interview with Peel about the possibility of an afterlife, and Faithful was asked whether she had ever thought 'somebody' was looking after her, but otherwise the spiritual content was rather vague.

Religious documentaries

A documentary is a factual film or television programme about an event or person. It may be presented from one point of view — if the presenter wants to show his or her support or otherwise for the subject of the programme — or it may be a straightforward presentation of information. Religious documentaries are increasingly popular, especially on Channels 4 and 5. They are targeted mainly at those who are 'vaguely religious' rather than at the religious believer. This may include people with a general or academic interest in religion but no personal commitment. The questions addressed are often ones of everyday interest: What is the best explanation for the existence of the world and its features? What is the purpose of humans? How should we behave towards others and the world around us? Sometimes the presenters talk to controversial figures in the religious world, or challenge issues of moral and religious belief and practice.

As part of its dedicated Texas series, in January 2004 Channel 4 showed an episode on *Teenage Texan Virgins*. In the famously religious state, teenagers are being encouraged to take purity pledges — vows of chastity — committing them to nothing more intimate than kissing before marriage. Those who have failed to live up to this high expectation are made to feel guilty and impure. 'You wouldn't want to put a toothbrush in your mouth that someone else had used,' says the preacher.

Sex in marriage is like a fire in a fireplace. Sex outside marriage is like a fire in the middle of the floor: it burns the house down and destroys everything. In terrifying tones [the preacher] described the alleged wages of sin: sex brings disease; condoms have holes in them.

The Silver Ring Thing encourages chastity until marriage

The power of the Church in Texas is such that the law prohibits sex education in the belief that this will discourage teenagers from pre-marital sex. They are taught that condoms are faulty and that they will probably die from painful sexually transmitted diseases if they engage in anything other than kissing. Teaching is aimed at making teenagers fearful and keeping them in ignorance, which has led to Texas having the highest rate of teenage pregnancies in the USA. The Texas Health Department believes it is fighting a losing battle if it cannot get into churches and correct the misinformation being spread to young people.

Another Channel 4 documentary in the same series, *Turning Muslim in Texas* (January 2004), observed that Islam is the fastest-growing religion in the USA. Texas is home to 400,000 Muslims, many of whom are converts from Christianity. Eric, a former Baptist, stated: 'Islam is everything I wanted Christianity to be.' Even the strict, Bible-belt Christianity of Texas did not give him the security of a faith that provides specific guidance on every aspect of daily life. Yasmine, a former business executive, believes Islam is the solution to the moral evils of the age. Muslim converts have a special role to play

Muslims meet to worship in Austin, Texas

in helping those who have been brought up as Muslims to get back to the fundamentals of the faith. David, who converted while in the US army, arranged a marriage to a Moroccan native Muslim who was surprised by how strictly he expected her to follow the Qur'an — she now wears a hijab, as does their daughter.

The converts all commented that since 11 September 2001 there has been an increasing interest in Islam among Americans who are seeking to find out what the religion really teaches and not just how the popular media present it. David suggested that converting to Islam could save Americans from themselves and that if George W. Bush converted, it would discourage him from some of his 'ill-advised imperial adventures overseas'.

Miracles was a one-off religious documentary shown on Channel 4 in 2001, which followed the work of Benny Hinn and Reinhardt Bonnke, two internationally renowned evangelists. The documentary team had access to all their miracle crusades in the mid-west USA and Nigeria over the period of a year, and followed up those who had claimed to be healed. It was clear that the documentary team was very sceptical, and the presentation of the work of both men was savagely critical. Allegedly, no healings could be followed up in Nigeria due to the lack of medical records, and of over 70 healings claimed at Hinn's crusade in Portland, Oregon, only a few names were fed back to the documentary team. None of the healings could be proved, and in one sad case, a woman who believed she had been cured of cancer died 9 months later. At the end of one of Bonnke's crusades, several people were trampled to death as they left and the father of one dead girl laid her body on the bonnet of Bonnke's Mercedes in the hope that she would be raised from the dead.

Although the programme was highly critical, it also showed how many people were deeply committed to Hinn's ministry. The team followed the case of Ashneel Prakash, the 10-year-old younger son of recent immigrants and converts to Christianity through the ministry of Benny Hinn. Ashneel had multiple brain tumours and a terminal diagnosis, but his parents were sure he would be healed at one of Hinn's meetings. Even after the boy died, having received special prayers from Hinn, his parents, although grief stricken, were still committed to Hinn and his ministry.

The programme followed up on research carried out by the American neurologist, Professor Michael Persinger, who had copied in the laboratory the conditions generated at a miracle crusade — bright lights and music. His subjects all reported feelings like those of a religious experience, even though they knew they had been part of a scientific experiment. Experts who appeared on the programme also compared the methods used by Hinn and Bonnke to those used by Hitler: stirring up crowds to mass excitement and encouraging them to do things they would not normally do.

Running for God was shown on ITV1 in 2003. It followed the fortunes of three Christian women hurdlers as they prepared for the Commonwealth Games and examined the relationship between their faith and their sporting talents. By the end of the programme, all three had either been forced by injury or ill health to withdraw from the games, or failed to qualify due to poor performance. Inevitably, the question was left in the viewer's mind whether their faith had served any useful purpose for them.

God Bless America was shown on Channel 4 in November 2004 as the race for the US presidency drew to a close. It examined how the 'religious right' in the USA had emerged powerfully in the wake of the Watergate scandal. The 'religious right' was concerned with cleaning up politics and believed Christian values were the way to restore America's morality. Jimmy Carter made as much of his religious views as his political ones, but still failed the test of the moral majority for being too left wing. The 'religious right' had a powerful effect not only on sexual matters but also on foreign policy, and claimed credit for the defeat of the liberal democrats in the Reagan era. Nonetheless, members of the 'religious right' are committed in their hatred of homosexuals (arguing that AIDS is a punishment from God), want all abortion banned, and are utterly opposed to homosexual marriages.

In 1988, the Christian Coalition member, Rev Pat Robertson, stood against George Bush Sr and has since continued to exhibit considerable power and control over many state Republican parties. However, the Coalition has failed to impose its Christian values on the American legal system. Moral issues continue to be highly politicised in the USA, although George W. Bush, who claims to have become a Christian at the age of 40 after a period of alcoholism and drug addiction, played down his Christianity to gain votes.

Bush was re-elected to a second term at the White House 4 days after this documentary was shown, with the media highlighting the fact that he had done so because he was supported by the increasing number of Evangelical Christians in the USA.

The Big Question: Why Are We Here? was shown on Channel 5 in spring 2004. Presented by Richard Dawkins, the popular atheist scientist, it addressed the question of why human beings are so keen to answer the question 'why are we here?', considering both religious and scientific answers. Dawkins looked at the work of William Paley who, in 1802, put forward the example of the watch and the watchmaker (see page 13). According to Paley, the complex design of the universe could only be explained by reference to God. Dawkins, however, disagreed. He put forward an argument about natural selection to claim that human beings see purpose in the universe when it is not actually there, still less designed by God. He suggested instead that purpose exists in human beings themselves.

Satellite and cable stations

Satellite and cable television now offer a vast range of religious broadcasting, most of which comes from the USA. It is available 24 hours a day, and includes televised services, sermons, Bible teaching, evangelistic rallies or talks by leading Christian speakers and ministers. Televangelism is a multi-million dollar industry in the USA and many people come into contact with Christianity for the first time through watching religious broadcasts, which are transmitted all over the world. Many radio and television stations in the USA are owned by Churches that run their own programmes — some very glitzy and expensive, others working to a much lower budget, relying largely on televising their regular church services. If you still think that religion is for people who wear old-fashioned clothes and sing hymns by dead hymn writers, spend a couple of

Church services are popular material for satellite stations

hours surfing the religious channels on Sky or another satellite service provider. Your eyes may be opened to another side of religious life and worship altogether.

Religious and moral issues in film

Although few feature films are made with the deliberate intention of unpacking religious themes, religious and moral themes do emerge in films in mainstream cinema. Occasionally, a film captures the public's interest when it has at its heart religious, moral and ethical issues. It is not just religious believers who are interested in these issues, as they touch on matters relevant to everyone — the sanctity of life, sexual relationships, medical technology, and the power of religion to shape people's thoughts and ideas.

In most cases, the religious or moral theme of a film is presented alongside the more usual subjects of popular film — romance, family dramas, adventures and murders, war and political intrigues, science fiction and fantasy. It is worth considering whether it should be the function of a feature film to examine moral, ethical or religious issues, or to entertain. If its function is to entertain, does this mean directors cannot convey any opinions on ethical issues? Is it the role of film directors to make their audience think, and perhaps to impose their opinion on the viewer, or should they be impartial?

Gattaca (15)

(1997; Director: Andrew Nichol; starring Ethan Hawke and Jude Law)

This Hollywood blockbuster directly challenges a very real ethical issue: the potential that has been unleashed by genetic engineering. The film opens with a biblical verse running across the screen: 'Consider God's handiwork. Who can straighten what he has made crooked?' (Ecclesiastes 7:13). Although it is a futuristic film, it is set in a 'not too distant future', in which responsible parents do not leave it to God to determine the future of their offspring. Instead, prospective parents ask their local geneticist to engineer a 'perfect' embryo: 'Ten fingers and ten toes — that's all that used to matter. Not now.' This is a world in which women take swabs of their lips to catch the saliva from a potential husband's kiss in order to have the DNA analysed — to assess the positive and negative attributes — and in which children destined by their parents to be pianists are genetically engineered with an extra finger on each hand so they can play pieces 'that can only be played with twelve fingers'.

The hero of the film, Vincent, was not genetically engineered. He was a 'faith birth' or 'God birth', conceived not in a laboratory but in the back of a Detroit Riviera. As such, he is destined to be an 'in-valid'. His life expectancy is a mere 30 years and he suffers from short-sightedness and a heart defect. His genetic CV determines every choice he has to make. Those with imperfect profiles are destined to a life of misery, drifting from one menial job to another: 'My real résumé was in my cells.... We now have discrimination down to a science.'

His younger brother, Anton, however, is genetically engineered to have 'hazel eyes, dark hair and fair skin' and the geneticist reassures his parents that he has 'eliminated any potentially prejudicial conditions — myopia [short-sightedness], baldness, alcoholism'. When his parents ask whether they should perhaps leave some things to chance, the geneticist advises: 'You want to give your child the best possible start. Believe me, we have enough imperfections built in already. Your child doesn't need any additional burdens.'

While Anton is favoured by his parents — 'A child my father considered worthy of his name' — Vincent is brought up to expect very little and his burning ambition to go into space is thwarted at every turn: 'The only way you'll see the inside of a spaceship is if you are cleaning it.' One day, when he beats Anton in a regular swimming dare that he usually fails, he realises that he does not have to accept the fate his poor genes have determined. Working outside the law, he courageously challenges the system and, via a black-market broker of DNA, he enters into a partnership with Jerome Morrow, a former swimming star with 'an IQ off the register...the heart of an ox.... You could go anywhere with this guy's helix tucked under your arm.' Jerome is in a wheelchair, paralysed by a road accident, bitter and alcoholic. Jerome's fate reveals the real-life tragedies behind the system: 'For the genetically superior, success is easier to obtain, but it is by no means guaranteed. There is no gene for fate, and when the elite fall on hard times, their genetic identity becomes a valuable commodity for the unscrupulous.'

Taking on Jerome's identity, using his blood, skin, urine and skin samples to pass the identity tests, Vincent enters the space agency, Gattaca, and eventually achieves his ambition to be part of a space mission to Titan. Ironically, in the closing minutes of the film, it emerges that the doctor who always checked Vincent's samples had never been fooled. He had kept quiet about the fraud since his own son was genetically imperfect and yet lived with the same hope that Vincent had harboured — that he could overcome his genetic imperfection to fulfil his dreams.

Sadly, Jerome commits suicide. He has fulfilled his usefulness in providing Vincent with the means to enter Gattaca, but he has never been able to deal with the 'burden of perfection'. We learn that he had never come to terms with winning only a silver swimming medal, and that his disability was the result of a suicide attempt, not a random car accident.

The film raises the question: what happens when man takes God's authority to determine life, death and human destiny? Both Vincent and Jerome emerge as victims of the system. Neither is free; both are controlled by their genetic profile.

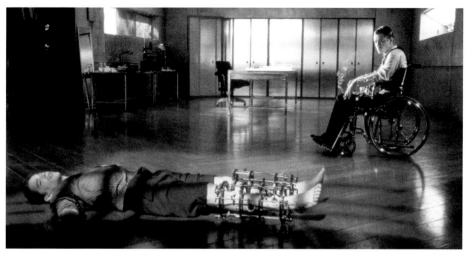

Vincent goes to extreme lengths to take on the identity of 'valid' Jerome Morrow

Priest (15)

(1994; Director: Antonia Bird; starring Linus Roache, Robert Carlyle and Tom Wilkinson)

One of the most interesting and heartwarming films that directly tackles a religious issue is *Priest*. This deals with the enormous emotional, moral and spiritual problems faced by Greg, a young, gay Catholic priest working in a rough, poverty-stricken parish in inner-city Liverpool. He believes that the role of the priest should be to set a pristine moral example to his parishioners, and he is shocked to find that his boss, the liberal, socially-conscious Matthew, is conducting a loving sexual relationship with Maria, their housekeeper. Catholic priests are bound by rules of celibacy, and Greg thinks Matthew is hypocritical, preaching against social sins to his congregation while living a double life in private: 'You can't change the rules just because they don't suit you. There's just sin,' he tells Matthew. Matthew clearly feels that Greg is pompous and naive, passing judgements he is not entitled to pass, and only later do we discover that Greg has his own problems to deal with.

The parish is a challenge to Greg — the parishioners are often drunk and aggressive — and his ideals are soon shattered. Matthew is able to relate to

Father Greg Pilkington struggles to keep his vow of celibacy

his parishioners on their level, knowing they have little need for theology but a great need for someone who can identify with them in their joys and sorrows. Greg is appalled to witness Matthew singing karaoke in the local pub, and accuses him of being undignified. After a wake following the funeral of a parishioner, Greg visits a gay bar in the city, where he meets Graham. They begin an uneasy relationship, spoiled by Greg's guilt and pain as he lives in fear of being uncovered but also struggles hugely with the conflict between his calling to the priesthood and his natural sexual inclinations.

He faces further problems when 14-year-old Lisa tells him that her father has been sexually abusing her. Greg is not allowed to tell social services or Lisa's mother. When the truth is uncovered, Lisa's mother finds it impossible to forgive Greg.

Eventually, Greg is 'outed' as a homosexual and forced into exile in a hostile, remote parish. Matthew is determined to bring Greg back to the parish and attempts to persuade him that he has not committed the unforgivable sin.

> *Matthew:* You've broken a manmade rule, that's all.
> *Greg:* The Church gives us everything…and all she asks in return is celibacy.
> *Matthew:* Christ didn't ask us to be celibate.

Greg, however, is convinced that homosexuality is in every way a sin and a sickness. Eventually, he is persuaded to return to the parish, and Matthew makes clear to his congregation that he expects Greg to be received with compassion. The 'sin' of homosexuality is, for Matthew, nothing compared to the hypocritical morality he sees enacted by the Church: 'When I see careerists, hypocrites and Pharisees in the Church, then I doubt the existence of God. How could he let that happen?' Greg's return to the parish does not go smoothly. The Church is violently divided, and many refuse to take communion from him, shouting abuse at both priests. Only Lisa, who Greg feels he has let down so badly, is able to understand his pain, and the film ends as she alone stands in line to receive the sacrament from him.

Priest needs to be watched sensitively. It paints a touching portrait of the pain that arises from separating the calling to be a priest from the person that priest is — in Greg's case, a homosexual priest, and in Matthew's, a heterosexual priest who cannot accept that Church doctrine has the genuine authority to prevent him having a loving relationship with a woman. Neither is naturally suited to the priesthood and yet both are gifted and convinced of their calling.

Yentl (PG)

(1983; Director: Barbra Streisand; starring Barbra Streisand and Nehemiah Persoff)

This film includes beautiful songs and tells the story of a young Jewish woman at the beginning of the twentieth century who, after the death of her father, rebels against the ruling that women cannot study the Torah (the Jewish law). She disguises herself as a boy and enters a Jewish college, becoming one of its brightest students. Inevitably, it is eventually revealed that she is a woman, and although there are romantic elements to the plot, which may seem irrelevant, they are used to draw attention to the assumptions made about male and female roles in this very traditional religious society.

Religious and moral issues in UK soap operas

Soaps originated in the American radio serials of the 1930s, which were sponsored by soap powder companies. Television soap operas are long-running serials concerned with everyday life, in which multiple storylines are carried over from one episode to the next. Successful soaps run for many years and new viewers have to be able to join in at any stage. The passage of time also appears to reflect real time for the viewers and in long-running soaps the characters age as the viewers do. Soaps sometimes deal with topical events in the world outside the programmes and their emphasis is on social problems. Events in soap operas include courtships, marriages, divorces, deaths and disappearances. Gossip is a key feature in soaps and any important information that a viewer might have missed is worked into the conversation, but knowledge of previous events is useful. Relationships are more important than events and soaps do not need to have a beginning, middle and end. There is no one dominant story line, but several stories are linked together over a limitless number of episodes. The focus of interest is always on how events affect characters rather than the events themselves.

Because soaps are concerned with human issues and how they affect people, they provide a huge amount of material for discussion. Soap plots are ever-changing, so when studying one of them do not rely on an old storyline you did not actually see and have simply read about. Set out to watch or video one soap regularly over a period of 4 weeks and you will soon have plenty of new material to use in your exam or coursework.

Eastenders

Eastenders, a BBC production, was first broadcast in 1985. Its makers intended it to be realistic and to reflect everyday life. The then producer, Julia Smith, said: 'We decided to go for a realistic, fairly outspoken type of drama which could encompass stories about homosexuals, rape, unemployment, racial prejudice etc. in a believable context.' The characters tend to be mainly working class, and when characters from outside that social group, e.g. barristers, are presented, they are often stereotypes. Women, young people and men are given strong roles, so the potential audience is wide, and issues covered are relevant to all ages, genders and circumstances. Issues addressed on *Eastenders* have included:

- single-parent families
- prostitution
- attempted suicide
- alcoholism
- cot death
- poverty
- mental breakdown

- teenage pregnancy
- arranged marriages
- drug problems
- organised crime
- extra-marital affairs and marital conflict
- murder and suspected murder

It was part of the intention of the programme-makers to handle controversial social issues. As a result, *Eastenders* is, to some degree, educational and informative. If a particular issue has been addressed by an episode, a helpline phone number is often displayed at the end, so people who have been affected by the same issue can get support or extra information.

Casualty, *Holby City* and *The Bill*

Casualty, *Holby City* and *The Bill* belong to the category of drama series known as 'institutional drama'. They are set within a closely defined area of a hospital or police station, and rarely take the viewer outside those confines. The plot intertwines ongoing stories about the lives of the people who work there with plots that are specific to each episode. In recent years, these institutional dramas have acquired the characteristics of soap operas by including stories about leading characters. However, unlike traditional soaps, there is more scope for plots which are not continued from one episode to the next. Issues covered in these programmes include:

- gambling
- drug addiction
- surrogacy
- infidelity
- stalking
- child abuse
- abduction
- workplace bullying
- alcoholism
- bereavement
- bigamy
- murder
- incest
- homosexual partnerships

Religious and moral issues in the news media

Ethical and moral issues dominate newspaper reporting. Look at a newspaper regularly over the course of a month and you will see a range of articles every day which could be useful to your studies. Because there are so many newspapers with different styles, you can look at how an ethical issue is covered from several angles. Do not use just one type of paper — look at tabloids and broadsheet newspapers, both during the week and at the weekend. Weekend newspapers often devote more space to discussion of ethical issues. Each newspaper usually has a predictable response to most issues, depending on its readership. While some newspapers are more open about offering an opinion, others appear to be unbiased, although contributions from medical, legal or academic experts present the case from differing perspectives.

Once you have chosen the issue and article you want to write about, use a checklist to guide you through your answer. You could include the following:

- Consistency with other articles: how does the article fit into the style and approach of the paper as a whole?
- Language and style: is the article written to arouse readers' emotions, to make them angry or sad, or to encourage them to do something in response — donating money to a relevant charity, for example?
- Readership: how does the article aim to reach its target audience? Compare how the *Sun* and *The Times* might address the issue of homosexual marriage, for example.
- Use of headlines: are they intended to shock, amuse, puzzle or alarm?
- Use of pictures: are these designed to make the reader feel touched, inspired, horrified or amused?

Newspapers are an important source of information about the world

You should also critically evaluate the way in which the newspaper has handled the issue. Make sure you use evaluative language and offer clear reasons why you think it could have handled the issue more effectively.

Questions and activities

Sample questions and answers

The sample answers given here are examples of the type of answer you should write if you are doing the coursework option. They are therefore longer than you would be expected to write in the exam.

1 Describe the variety of religious programmes broadcast on terrestrial television channels. (4 marks)

Religious broadcasting is a legal requirement and, although terrestrial television channels do not offer as much religious broadcasting as they do other areas, such as sport or entertainment, there is a surprisingly wide range of religious programmes available on all terrestrial channels. Specifically religious programmes are essentially divided into two categories: worship and magazine programmes/religious documentaries. To be specifically religious, the programme must be aimed at least at a 'vaguely religious' audience and the religious theme must be dominant throughout.

Worship and magazine programmes include *Songs of Praise* and *The Heaven and Earth Show*. *Songs of Praise* is a weekly programme broadcast early on Sunday evening. It includes worship songs and hymns from different congregations each week, as well as magazine items focusing on Christians in the area, Church projects and solo musical items. The heart of the programme is Christian music, but it includes items of human interest. *The Heaven and Earth Show* is also a magazine programme, shown on Sunday mornings, which covers a wide range of issues of belief in the modern day. It includes articles about issues relevant to all the major faiths and to New Age spirituality. It is presented in a contemporary format and encourages participation from the studio audience and from viewers at home.

Channel 4 offers a range of programmes that are of interest to religious believers. These include programmes about death, evil, black theology and the issues raised by being a Muslim in Britain. A Channel 4 team even followed Muslims going on Hajj. In August 2003, the station presented a series of four programmes called *Some of my Best Friends are…*, featuring religious believers from Catholic, Muslim, Anglican and Jewish backgrounds. These programmes tackled serious contemporary issues raised within the different faiths. For example, in *Some of my Best Friends are Muslim*, Yasmin Alibhai Brown talked about polygamy, hijabs, and the threats made against her and others who were thought to be challenging traditional Islam.

Religious documentaries appear on all the main channels. They cover everything from the lives of prominent modern-day Christians to dramatic reconstructions of the lives of biblical characters. For example, a recent series aimed to reconstruct the life and role of Mary, examining common rumours such as that she was raped by a Roman soldier. Another programme followed the life of Moses and examined the ten plagues, offering natural explanations for them. *Running for God* looked at the lives of three Christian women who were preparing to run in the Commonwealth Games, and investigated the role their faith played in their approach to sport. These were one-off programmes, but some appear more regularly. *Witness* on Channel 4 is screened at regular intervals, and deals with often controversial issues within religion, aiming to cover 'a range of stories that collide with faith, identity and belief'.

2 Discuss the ways in which an issue of moral concern to Christians is dealt with in national newspapers. (8 marks)

The four newspapers we looked at (the *Sun*, the *Daily Mail*, *The Times* and the *Independent*) dealt with the moral issues raised by the death of Harold Shipman, focusing on two particular concerns for Christians: suicide and justice. For Christians, suicide is an issue of moral concern, because many see it as an act of rebellion against God's gift of life. Justice is important for Christians because God is just, and ideally things in life should be fair and equal. In particular, the question was raised of whether Shipman had escaped justice by committing suicide.

The article in the *Sun* was written in a vengeful tone. We saw this in a small section at the bottom of one page about Sarah Payne's killer, effectively encouraging him to follow Shipman's example. The writer clearly wants the reader to hate Shipman and communicates this using emotive language. The article does not contain much information on the subject matter, but, using big headlines and pictures, the reader gains all the information about how Shipman killed himself. The article suggests that relatives of Shipman's victims are not happy he has died, but are angry because they feel he has cheated the system by avoiding completing his life sentence. Now they will never have the chance to find out his motives for committing so many murders. The *Sun* articles were placed next to sexually suggestive pictures and articles, which I felt lowered the seriousness of the issue. The emphasis was on celebrating his death, rather than finding out how Shipman had managed to commit suicide in prison and whether anyone should be accountable for that.

The first thing I noticed about the *Daily Mail* article on Shipman's death was the headline: 'Dr Death played God to the end'. I think this is a powerful title as it uses religious imagery, and it assumes that such language will be understandable even to non-religious readers. The article is much more informative than the *Sun*, and uses much less emotive writing. However, it does place more emphasis on the fact that justice has not been done. It includes a section on Shipman's wife, which shows some sympathy for her, headlined: 'She refuses to face the truth'. A diagram shows how Shipman managed to kill himself and the piece is supported by an article on suicide rates in prison.

The Times has an even more moderate headline, which does not even include the fact that Shipman is dead. The reader has to read the article to extract that information.

A photo of one of his victims and her husband generates sympathy for the partner left behind. The incident is not tackled in detail until well into the body of the paper and the articles are analytical, including one written by a psychologist, one about the need for the government to exercise greater controls over GPs, and another about the measures used in prisons to prevent suicides among prisoners.

The *Independent* does not have any headline at all about Shipman's death. The reader has to wait to page 4 to find anything on the incident. However, there is a clever photograph, which shows only Shipman's eyes and nose, and which looks very menacing. The article is tightly packed and includes a lot of information in a small font, which makes it slower to digest than the *Sun* or the *Daily Mail*.

All of the newspapers are interested in the psychology behind Shipman's actions, stressing that the mystery of his motives will now not be solved. Shipman chose the moment of his death as he did not permit his victims to do, and it is clear that all the papers felt he had violated the principle of justice in this way, and had not paid the true penalty for his crimes. The moral law had not been served. Christians are also concerned about the increased number of suicides as a sign that society is letting down its most vulnerable members. Until comparatively recently, the attempt to commit suicide was technically illegal, and a successful suicide would not be buried in consecrated ground. Many Christians believed that anyone who committed suicide would go straight to hell. However, most Christians are now more sympathetic towards the anguish suffered by people who commit suicide.

3 'Television programmes fail to show religious believers as having any serious contribution to make to society.' Do you agree? Give reasons for your opinion, showing you have considered another point of view. Your answer should refer to specific television programmes.   (8 marks)

I do not agree with this statement, as there is far more religious broadcasting than we might first think, and most of it deals with religious people in a fair and unbiased way. However, a minority of programmes fail to do so and it is easy to see why they may lead people to this opinion.

Most religious broadcasting deals with religious people's faith as having significance, not only to them but to society as a whole. Programmes that examine sophisticated religious and philosophical themes, such as *Soul Searching*, which examined questions about the soul — whether it exists, whether God placed it there — do not trivialise religion. They expose important issues that are not of concern just to religious believers but to all humans. Religious documentaries usually take an academic position on the subjects they are discussing, and although they may not come up with a conclusion that all religious people would agree with (that would be virtually impossible, anyway), they present their evidence in a fair way. They recognise that for religious believers there are important implications in, for example, attempting to prove the resurrection, or, as *Everyman* does, examining moral and religious issues such as inter-faith marriages or euthanasia.

However, there are some programmes that are biased in their approach. We watched a video of a documentary shown on Channel 4 in 2000 called *Miracles*. This followed the work of the international evangelist Benny Hinn, who is the focus of huge rallies or crusades where people come expecting to be healed from cancer, arthritis, paralysis or brain damage. Although the programme showed some people who were genuinely committed to Hinn's work and were expecting a miracle to happen, it adopted a sceptical position and effectively accused Hinn of being a fraud who practised hypnosis on the crowds that came to his crusades. Interestingly, the programme-makers used religious figures as well as psychologists to criticise Hinn, which may have given an illusion of fairness, but it seemed they had already made up their minds and were not really examining all the evidence. In this case, it was clear that the programme did not intend the viewer to think that religious people had anything valuable to offer society.

Another problem in the presentation of religious people is the way they are sometimes depicted in dramas and soaps. Soap operas, such as *Eastenders*, rarely include a character who is a genuine religious believer, but rather someone who is nominally religious or a caricature of a believer, such as Dot Cotton. She is presented as being judgemental and intolerant, quoting Bible verses out of context. When she had a crisis of faith after being mugged, the programme did not show her as belonging to a community of fellow believers who could support her, but as being rather isolated. This does not reflect the life and attitudes of most modern Christians, and can lead to a negative view of the contribution they can make to society. On the other hand, when she was diagnosed with cancer, she approached her operation trusting in God, and she seemed much more genuine. Since many people only ever encounter a

Christian on television rather than in their own life, it is important that Christians are presented as being genuine people, not stereotypes.

Overall, I think that although some television programmes show religious believers as having nothing useful to offer society, many religious programmes try to show this is not universally true. Even though people may not be interested in following religious practices, there is a genuine interest in religious, ethical and spiritual issues, and this comes across in many television programmes which include some valuable contributions from religious people. It tends to be in soap operas, comedy shows and popular dramas that religious people are presented as irrelevant or irritating, not in documentaries or other fact-based programmes.

Class activities and homework

Understanding the media

In pairs or small groups look at different popular magazines that deal with television, film and 'celebrity' issues. Put together a presentation for the rest of the class on issues you find which could be of concern to religious believers. In your presentation, consider what messages the magazine articles send out to their readers and whether they support religious moral principles. If not, does it matter? If so, consider why, given that their readership will be predominantly non-religious? Under your teacher's guidance, discuss these issues with the rest of the class.

Understanding religious broadcasting

Your teacher will show you a compilation video tape of a range of specifically religious television programmes. Under your teacher's guidance, discuss the issues covered in the programmes and the way in which they are communicated to the viewer. Pay special attention to the difference, if any, between programmes likely to be watched by mostly religious viewers, and those that address a specifically religious issue but are aimed at a wider audience.

Watch one specifically religious television programme on one of the terrestrial channels. Prepare a presentation, including a handout, for the rest of the class for a future lesson.

Understanding religious and ethical issues in films

Over the course of several lessons, your teacher will show you a film that deals with a major moral or religious issue and guide you in an extensive discussion on the matters it raises. Make sure you write proper notes, or use the handout your teacher gives you, to guide your discussion.

Examine the ways in which a religious or moral issue has been tackled in a film or television drama.

Understanding religious and ethical issues in soap operas

Your teacher will show you several episodes of a soap opera, identifying key excerpts that either address a range of ethical issues or unpack a long-running issue over the course of several episodes. As a class, discuss how the issue(s) is treated.

Find out about the ethical issues that have been covered in *Coronation Street* (or another soap, if you have covered this one already in class) over the years. This is a very long-running soap and offers a considerable range of controversial issues. Remember, however, that you have to be able to write about the issues in some depth.

Would it be realistic or useful for religious believers to become more involved in writing and making soap operas? Do you think soap operas reflect the real state of religious belief in the UK or do they underestimate how many people are committed to a religious faith?

Understanding the presentation of moral or religious issues in newspapers

Collect a range of daily newspapers that cover the same moral issue. As a class, examine and discuss the different ways in which the issue is presented. In pairs or small groups, write a newspaper article addressing the issue from an entirely religious perspective. How different are these articles from the originals? Would they be publishable in a national newspaper? Consider why this may or may not be the case.

Create a collage of headlines, pictures and articles from different newspapers which highlight the various ways they present a religious or moral issue. Annotate the collage to draw attention to key features in the different accounts.

Religion, wealth and poverty

The nature of wealth and poverty

Christian teaching on wealth

> For the love of money is a root to all kinds of evil.
>
> (1 Timothy 6:10)
>
> True happiness is not found in riches.
>
> (Catechism of the Catholic Church)

The Bible teaches that **wealth** can be a dangerous thing. People begin to desire more and more money and possessions and it is easy for money to become the most important thing in people's lives. They may love and worship wealth more than God. The problem with being wealthy is that people believe money will solve all their problems and make them happy.

You cannot serve both God and Money.   (Matthew 6:24)

It is easier for a camel to go through the eye of a needle than for a rich man to enter the kingdom of God.
(Mark 10:25)

Wealth
Money, land
and possessions

Being wealthy means having money, land or expensive possessions and, with wealth, often comes power. In the UK, people may be wealthy for a number of reasons. For example, they may have highly paid jobs, they may have inherited wealth from their families or they may have gained it through business or investments and speculation on the stock market. A few have become wealthy through winning the National Lottery. Many religious believers are concerned about the National Lottery because it is a form of gambling. Although the lottery is apparently less dangerous and addictive than casino gambling because it is so public, many people are prepared to leave themselves without enough money to buy food and clothes because they would rather chance another lottery ticket.

Being wealthy is *not* against Christian teaching, but greed for possessions is. In Western society, people are constantly encouraged to believe that getting more and more money and possessions is a good thing — look at the popularity of programmes such as *Who Wants to Be a Millionaire?* Prize money in game shows is rising all the time, and what people are prepared to do to win it is becoming increasingly bizarre and often humiliating.

Used wrongly, wealth can be a dangerous thing — it is easy for rich people to feel they have everything, and to fail to acknowledge and worship God. Instead, they seek more money and material possessions, and money becomes their God because it is what they trust and rely on most. In the parable of the rich fool (Luke 12:13–21), Jesus explains that storing up lots of money and possessions on earth will be of no use to us when we die. It is better to be rich before God, by doing good deeds and acting with love towards others. In the Sermon on the Mount, Jesus taught: 'Do not store up for yourselves treasures on earth, where moth and rust destroy, and where thieves break in and steal. But store up for yourselves treasures in heaven' (Matthew 6:19–20).

Christians believe wealth is a gift from God and should be used to help those less fortunate. People who have wealth are stewards and **stewardship** means taking care of money and using it responsibly. Many Christians feel it is important for the wealth of the world to be more fairly distributed, so that suffering may be relieved and all people may have a decent standard of living. In the parable of the sheep and the goats, Jesus said that when someone helps a person in need, they are actually helping Jesus himself:

> 'Lord, when did we see you hungry and feed you, or thirsty and give you something to drink…?' I tell you the truth, whatever you did for one of the least of these brothers of mine, you did for me.
>
> (Matthew 25:37,40)

> Go, sell everything you have and give it to the poor, and you will have treasure in heaven.
>
> (Mark 10:21)

The Bible teaches that it is a Christian duty to give money to the Church and to the poor. This is called **almsgiving** or charity. Helping those in need is at the centre of Jesus's teaching about loving one another. Some Christians do this by making a **tithe**. They set aside 10% of their income to give to the Church. They may also give extra offerings on top of this in response to particular needs that arise in their community or in the world. Some Churches make this an obligation on their members, while others leave it to individuals to make the choice. There is some controversy as to whether the tithe should be 10% of net (after tax) earnings, or 10% of gross earnings. Most Christians who tithe believe that God will bless their finances so that they never feel the loss of the tithe, but other Christians claim Jesus did away with the Old Testament principle of tithing: 'Woe to you, teachers of the law and Pharisees, you hypocrites! You give a tenth of your spices — mint, dill and cumin. But you have neglected the more important matters of love, justice, mercy and faithfulness' (Matthew 23:23).

In all cases, giving should be done secretly, and be between God and the individual only:

Key words

Almsgiving
Charitable donations

Stewardship
Taking care of something that does not belong to you.

Tithe
The Christian idea of committing 10% of income to the Church or another religious organisation

When you give alms, do not let your left hand know what your right hand is doing, so that your alms may be done in secret, and your Father who sees in secret will reward you.

(Matthew 6:3–4)

If anyone has material possessions and sees his brother in need but has no pity on him, how can the love of God be in him?

(1 John 3:17)

Key word

Moral responsibility
An obligation to help other people which the law cannot enforce

Christians believe wealth should only be obtained in a lawful and moral way — not by exploiting others, for example through crime, pornography or drugs. It is important for wealthy people to have the qualities of compassion and justice to offer to others. Greed and exploitation can ruin these qualities. Christians believe that wealth should be used for good purposes and that the wealthy have a **moral responsibility** to use their wealth to help the poor. Some believe God will judge people according to how much they have helped the poor.

The relationship between rich and poor is important. All Christian Churches say the rich should share what they have with the poor. The expression of such love and caring shows the equality of all human beings. The riches of the earth are for all and not just for the wealthy: 'The Church should concern itself…with the poor and needy' (Catechism of the Catholic Church).

The following passages in the New Testament are a useful source of Christian teaching on attitudes to money and resources:
- The parable of the sheep and goats (Matthew 25:31–46).
- The story of the rich young man (Mark 10:17–31).
- The widow's offering (Mark 12:41–44).
- The parable of the good Samaritan (Luke 10:25–37).
- The parable of the rich fool (Luke 12:13–21).
- The parable of the rich man and Lazarus (Luke 16:19–31).

Christian teaching on poverty

Poverty is a lack of wealth and power. There are different kinds of poverty — it is not just the absence of money and material possessions. Poverty can also be a spiritual or emotional state, in which people lack self-respect and love.

What makes people wealthy or poor can depend on where they live. In the UK, people are rich if they have lots of money and poor if they have or earn much less. This is called **relative poverty**. However, people with very little money might actually be considered wealthy in a country where other people have nothing and live in **absolute poverty**.

The Bible teaches that the poor are special to God: 'Blessed are the poor in spirit, for theirs is the kingdom of heaven' (Matthew 5:3). Wealth can take people away from God, and it is suggested that those who are poor are in a stronger position to grow closer to him. The most important factor is how wealth is used.

> God blesses those who come to the aid of the poor and rebukes those who turn away from them.
>
> (Catechism of the Catholic Church)

Today, Christians tend to see poverty as something that is not God's will and which they have an obligation to fight against. However, this was not always the case. In the past, the Church taught that the divisions caused by poverty and wealth were simply to be accepted. The famous hymn, *All Things Bright and Beautiful,* expressed this well, although significantly the following verse is not found in modern hymnbooks.

Key words

Absolute poverty
Condition in which people have no money, land or possessions

Relative poverty
Poverty in a society where most people have some money, land or possessions

Many people around the world live in difficult conditions

The rich man in his castle
The poor man at his gate
God made them high and lowly
And ordered their estate.

Islamic teaching on wealth and poverty

By no means will you attain to righteousness until you spend (in the way of Allah) out of that which you cherish most.

(Surah 3:91)

The third pillar of Islam is Zakah — the religious tax that is an obligation upon all Muslims. This pillar provides the foundation for Muslim teaching on wealth and poverty, which is based on the belief that the universe and everything in it belongs to God. This includes all possessions and earnings, which are to be considered on loan or held in trust on behalf of God. Acts of charity or sacrifice are effectively giving back to the rightful owner what was temporarily in our possession.

Zakah is the third pillar of Islam

Wealth or poverty are conditions determined by God. Those lucky enough to be granted wealth have an obligation to give to relieve others' poverty. This is done is two ways. Zakah is regular, sacrificial giving that is not dependent on feeling sympathy or pity. Giving to world disasters or other specific concerns is called sadaqah, and occurs in addition to the duty of giving Zakah. Giving has implications for the afterlife:

Those who are saved from their own greed shall be the successful.

(Surah 64:16)

Spend your wealth for the cause of Allah, and do not be cast to ruin by your own hands; do good!

(Surah 2:195)

He is not a believer who eats his fill while his neighbour remains hungry by his side.

(Hadith)

Zakah amounts to 2.5% of a Muslim's income — not a huge amount, but because it is proportional to everyone's earnings, it is essentially just and fair. Zakah prevents greedy hoarding of money and resources, and keeps it circulating among those who need it while purifying (the meaning of the term 'Zakah') the giver. Greed, jealousy and hatred should be reduced by the regular cycle of giving and receiving through Zakah. The giver remembers that it is only by the grace of God that he is blessed with money to give in the first place. Islam is strictly opposed to charging interest on loans: the practice of giving loans serves to impose further financial burdens on the borrower and can lead to further abuses of the financial provisions so graciously given by God. Muslims are therefore encouraged to help the poor by giving interest-free loans or by offering money as a gift.

Zakah is given anonymously and is usually administered through the mosque. Many Muslims choose Ramadan as the season for giving Zakah, although others spread it out over the year. There is no way of checking up on whether a Muslim is obeying this third pillar. It is left to the individual and it is between them and God.

> Don't nullify your charity by reminders of your generosity, or by holding it against those you give it to — like those who give their wealth only to be seen by others…. They are like hard, barren rock on which is little soil. Heavy rain falls on it and leaves it just a bare stone.
>
> (Surah 2:264)

Zakah is given for the benefit of several groups, identified in Surah 9:60: the poor, those who work to administer Zakah, recent converts to Islam, slaves, debtors, missionaries of Islam, and 'wayfarers'.

Relief of poverty

In the UK, there are several reasons why people live in poverty. The most common reason is unemployment, which is often the result of a poor education and limited opportunities. Other causes include addiction to alcohol, drugs or gambling, which in turn can lead to homelessness and crime. The poor are also more likely to suffer ill health.

Key word

National poverty line
A measurement used by the UK government; those living below a certain level of income are said to live below the poverty line

According to recent figures, about a quarter of the population of the UK lives below the **national poverty line** — this is more than 13 million people, including 4 million children. About 3 million households have serious debt problems and 9 million people live in inadequate housing. The average national debt (excluding mortgages) in the UK at the end of 2004 was £17,000 per person. Given that some people have no debt at all, the amount that some people owe, while still being able to borrow more, is alarming. The most vulnerable to poverty are children and the families of the unemployed, ethnic minorities and asylum seekers.

In the UK, one of the big questions is: 'Who is responsible for the relief of poverty?' Does the government have an obligation to help those who are in situations of poverty or should it be left to local communities and charities? Those without work or other income may be entitled to unemployment benefit and other benefits provided by the state, such as the Working Families Tax Credit, but these funds can only supply the basics of life, not luxuries.

The Christian Churches are involved in the relief of poverty in the UK and there are a number of Christian social welfare agencies that promote policies to help those in need by encouraging discussions with the government. Other Christian help agencies include the Christian Alliance Housing Association, which helps young people and single parents to find safe and secure accommodation, and the Church Urban Fund, which supports community-based projects in poor areas. The Shaftesbury Society offers care and education for disadvantaged people and those with learning disabilities.

Christian organisations in the UK

The Leonard Cheshire Foundation

One famous Christian who worked tirelessly to help those in need in the UK was Leonard Cheshire. Born in 1917, Cheshire was a heroic bomber pilot in the Second World War and was awarded the Victoria Cross for bravery. Towards the end of the war, he watched the air raid on the Japanese city of Nagasaki in which an atomic bomb was dropped. He was so horrified by what he saw that he turned his life to saving people, rather than killing them.

Soon after the war, he discovered his old friend Arthur Dykes living in poverty and dying of a terminal illness. Arthur had nowhere to stay for his remaining few months, so Leonard invited Dykes to live with him in a large house Cheshire owned called Le Court. Cheshire learned some basic nursing skills and, soon after, took in another dying patient. More and more people heard about Cheshire's work and, soon after Arthur Dykes died, 24 terminally ill people came to stay at Le Court. Cheshire became a Catholic and set up the Leonard Cheshire Foundation, which provides homes for the terminally ill. Today it is the UK's largest disability care charity.

Leonard Cheshire

The Leonard Cheshire Foundation provides homes for 2,500 patients and offers a further 12,500 patients home care and **rehabilitation** visits. He once said that disabled people 'want to feel useful and need to find a purpose and a challenge to their lives, to have sufficient independence and the opportunity to lead a life of their own choosing.'

Key word

Rehabilitation
Equipping people, such as drug addicts, with the things they need to return to everyday life

The Salvation Army

The Salvation Army is the best-known Christian group helping the poor and needy in the UK. William Booth founded the organisation in 1865 to help the poor in inner cities. At first, Booth and his followers preached about Jesus in streets, pubs and music halls. They showed their love of Jesus in practical ways — by providing soup kitchens to feed the hungry and running hostels and shelters for homeless people and single mothers.

A Salvation Army officer

Today, the work of the Salvation Army continues in hostels for the homeless, and food and day centres for those who sleep on the streets. The organisation also helps the police and social services to find people who have gone missing. The Salvation Army runs rehabilitation centres for alcoholics and drug addicts, and campaigns vigorously against drugs and addiction. In Salvation Army churches (called citadels), there are clubs for young people and families, and centres for the very old.

The work of the Salvation Army is funded partly by the government and local authorities. It raises the rest of its money in three ways: street collections, special fund-raising events at Christmas and sales of its magazine, *The War Cry*. The mission statement of the Salvation Army is clear:

> The Salvation Army is an integral part of the universal Christian Church. Its message is based on the Bible, its motivation is the love of God as revealed in Jesus Christ. Its mission is to proclaim his gospel, to persuade people of all ages to become his disciples and to engage in a programme of practical concern for the needs of humanity.

The problem of world poverty

Many countries in the world are extremely wealthy; others are so poor that people regularly starve to death. The poorest countries in the world are called less economically developed countries (**LEDCs**). They need urgent and constant help from the more wealthy countries, but this has not always been forthcoming.

Key words

LEDCs
Less economically developed countries

World development
The need for rich and poor nations to work together to relieve world poverty

In 1980, the Brandt Report highlighted the huge differences between the rich and poor nations of the world. The report divided countries into three categories, according to their wealth:

- Developed countries: nations such as the USA, UK, the countries of western Europe, Japan and Australia, which are very wealthy.
- Developing countries: nations such as Brazil, Mexico and Malaysia, which are becoming richer.
- Less developed countries: including many African countries, which are extremely poor.

The developed countries contain only 25% of the world's population but own about 80% of the world's wealth. The Brandt Report called for the governments of all nations to seek a solution and highlighted the need for **world development** — a system of cooperation between rich and poor nations so that everyone can benefit.

There are many reasons why the less economically developed countries are so poor. The most common factors are:

- Debt: most poor countries have borrowed money from rich countries and find it difficult to pay them back; a huge amount of their very limited wealth is used to pay the debts.
- Cash crops: many poor countries have to grow cash crops such as cotton, tea and tobacco, which they can sell quickly to make money; these crops are grown on land that could be used to grow food for local people and this leads to starvation.
- Natural disasters: a number of poor countries suffer greatly from floods, droughts and earthquakes.
- Wars: a number of poor countries, particularly in Africa, are continually engaged in local wars caused by corruption and tribal or border disputes; these wars destroy crops and homes, leaving thousands of people without food or a place to live.
- Corrupt leaders: in many poor countries, the leadership is corrupt; the government does not distribute resources properly or fairly, but keeps them for itself or sells the country's precious resources in order to buy military equipment.
- Population growth: in the poorest countries, the population grows quickly and there are often too many people to feed and provide for; there is a lack of healthcare and education and many people die young.

The three poorest countries in the world in 2004 were Sierra Leone, Tanzania and Ethiopia. In each case, a family would have to live on less than £300 per year. In contrast, the three richest countries were Luxembourg, the USA and Switzerland, where the amount a family had to live on was over £18,000 per year.

For world development to occur, rich countries will have to reduce or cancel the debts owed to them by the poorer nations. A proper system of trade between rich and poor nations needs to be set up. The rich nations should not exploit the poor by paying very low prices for their goods and they should help the poorer nations to develop their

Famine affects millions of people throughout the world

agriculture and industry so that they do not have to rely on cash crops. This would be helpful to both sides — the poorer countries would become wealthier, which would mean that the rich countries would have new people and markets for their goods, and each side could help the other.

> Rich nations have a grave moral responsibility towards those which are unable to ensure the means of development by themselves.
>
> (Catechism of the Catholic Church)

The poorest countries, too, have to play their part in world development. It is the responsibility of the leaders of the poorer nations to stop corruption and ensure that the aid that is sent to their countries is used to help the poor. They also need to make a serious effort to put an end to the wars that constantly ravage the poorest areas.

The Christian response to world poverty

Christians believe that, just as God loves them, so they must love and care for their fellow human beings. Christianity teaches that all human life is precious and sacred to God (the principle of the sanctity of life).

An important development in recent years has been the growth within the Christian Church of Liberation Theology. This is a movement concerned with equality for all people. It believes that Christians must take positive action — even break the law — to fight against social injustice and the misuse of power by governments. The movement is strong in areas of poverty in Latin America, Africa and Asia.

The work of religious agencies

Christian Aid

> We will work with those who are committed to supporting poor and marginalised communities to eradicate poverty and promote basic rights and justice.
>
> (Christian Aid statement of intent)

The Christian Aid organisation was set up after the Second World War by the British Council of Churches to help people who were made homeless by the war and to help relieve poverty around the world. Its main aim is to help people to help themselves: 'We commit ourselves to strive for a new earth transformed by an end to poverty and to promote the dignity and basic rights of every person' (Christian Aid vision statement).

Christian Aid works with local experts in poor countries who know the local problems and the best way to deal with them. This has the added advantage of ensuring that the aid gets to the people who need it most. The charity raises money through donations, fund-raising and collections. For nearly 50 years, Christian Aid Week has been held in the UK every May. At that time, every household gets a letter from the organisation asking for donations to be put into a special envelope. This raises about £10 million every year. Christian Aid tries to show people why there is such a vital need to raise money to help the poorer nations. It sends its news magazine and other educational materials to schools and campaigns to raise public awareness of poverty around the world. Christian Aid also uses celebrities as its ambassadors in poorer countries.

Christian Aid week is supported by politicians and other public figures

Most of the money raised by Christian Aid is used on long-term aid, helping people out of poverty through **appropriate technology**. For example:

- In South America, farmers have been shown how to use modern and environmentally friendly farming methods.
- In Africa, Christian Aid has financed an agricultural school to teach farmers more efficient methods of producing food.
- In Afghanistan and elsewhere, Christian Aid workers have brought help to people made homeless by war.
- In the Middle East, Christian Aid has given help to Palestinians in the West Bank and Gaza Strip.
- In Bangladesh, Christian Aid has set up a factory to enable local people to make the medicines they need at a price they can afford.

Key word

Appropriate technology
Simple machinery and other tools that help people in the poorest parts of the world to improve their standard of living

The ethos of Christian Aid is that the best way to help the poor is to teach them how to look after themselves. This helps people to become self-reliant, with the skills and resources they need to break out of the cycle of poverty. As it declares: 'Give a man a fish: feed him for a day. Teach a man to fish: feed him for a lifetime.' Christian Aid has campaigned for the governments of rich nations to cancel the huge debts of the poorer nations and to encourage rich nations to buy the goods of poorer nations at a fair price.

About 15% of the money raised by Christian Aid is used for emergency aid. This is a disaster fund that is used in times of floods, earthquakes and wars to provide food, medicines, blankets and shelters for the victims. The incredible response to appeals from Christian Aid and many other organisations after the tsunami disaster in December 2004 (see page 20) showed how ready people are to respond to the needs of others. Hundreds of millions of pounds were raised in the UK alone to enable disaster relief and skilled staff to go to southeast Asia where people were suffering from homelessness, sickness, loss of livelihood and bereavement. It was interesting to see how people were drawn together in a spirit of compassion in quite an unprecedented way.

CAFOD

The Catholic Fund for Overseas Development (CAFOD) was founded in 1962 by the Catholic bishops of England and Wales. The aims of the organisation were to coordinate a large number of smaller charitable efforts together and to raise money. It raised £25,000 in the first year and, within 10 years, was helping 245 projects worldwide.

> CAFOD's mission is to promote human development and social justice in witness to Christian faith and Gospel values.
>
> (CAFOD mission statement)

Today, CAFOD is involved in over 1,000 poverty-relief programmes worldwide. About 65% of CAFOD's funding comes from donations from Catholic churches, groups and individuals, who raise almost £20 million a year. A further £10 million comes from governments and other donors. Like

Christian Aid, CAFOD places high importance on long-term development. In particular, CAFOD seeks to help the world's poor to develop agriculture, education and healthcare. It also provides immediate emergency help for people affected by wars, starvation and natural disasters.

CAFOD campaigns on behalf of the world's poor. Its officials have conducted in-depth studies into the causes of poverty, and have tried to get the richer nations to understand the problems of world poverty. In the last few years, CAFOD has campaigned for a total ban on landmines, and has argued that the rich nations should cancel the debt of the poorer nations.

CAFOD looks forward to a world in which...the voice of the poor is heard and heeded by all, and lives are no longer dominated by greed.

(CAFOD vision statement)

Mother Teresa of Calcutta

It is not how much we do, but how much love we put in the doing.

(Mother Teresa)

Mother Teresa was born Agnes Bojaxhiu in Skopje, Macedonia in 1910. She was raised in a poor Christian family. Her mother said the poor were God's special people and always insisted the family should share their food with other poor people. This had a great effect on young Agnes and, at the age of 17, she became a nun. She took on the religious name Teresa, and went to India to teach poor children.

On 10 September 1946, Teresa believed God called her to leave the convent to go and live among the destitute people of Calcutta. She had some basic medical training and, with the help of some volunteers, she went to Calcutta and set up a Christian community to help the poor.

Her work grew, and in 1952 Teresa opened the Nirmal Hriday Home for the Dying (the Place of the Pure Heart) and, soon after, a larger home called the Mother House. A little later, she opened a home for abandoned children and a special settlement was built where lepers could stay and receive medical treatment. Her volunteers were known as the Missionaries of Charity.

As the years passed, Mother Teresa became world famous for her work with the poor. She was the source of inspiration and hope to many people. She met the pope, the queen and many world leaders. In 1979, she received the Nobel peace prize. When she received the award, she remarked: 'I am grateful to receive the prize in the name of the hungry, the naked, the homeless, of the crippled, of the blind, of the lepers, of all those people who feel unloved.'

Today, the work of Mother Teresa continues in 80 countries. She died on 5 September 1997.

Muslim Aid

Muslim Aid was founded in 1985 and uses donations and legacies to aid millions of people in 50 of the poorest countries around the world. It responds to global emergencies, providing relief to victims of natural disasters, famine and war. The organisation also supports more long-term **development** programmes, such as provision of clean water, shelter, education and healthcare — tackling the root causes of poverty, not just its immediate effects. Muslim Aid is experienced in the field of international relief and development work. It works in partnership with local community-based organisations and helps local people to help themselves by giving them a sense of self-worth and dignity. Muslim Aid also runs offices in crisis areas, directly providing relief and development projects. It includes field offices in Sudan, Bangladesh and Somalia, which employ over 60 local staff. Since its establishment, Muslim Aid has helped people affected by war, famine, flooding, earthquakes and other natural disasters all over the world, including Palestine, Afghanistan, Bangladesh, Jamaica, Ethiopia, Angola, Bosnia, Chechnya, Kosova and Cambodia.

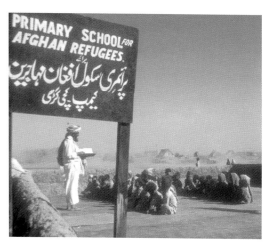

Providing education is a vital part of poverty relief

Key word

Development
Changes that improve people's lives

Questions and activities

Sample questions and answers

1 Outline Christian teaching about helping the poor and needy.

(4 marks)

Christianity teaches that the poor are special to God and that those who are wealthy should share what they have with the poor. Jesus taught that when people help someone in need, they are really helping him. He said: 'Whatever you did for one of the least of these brothers of mine, you did for me' (Matthew 24:40). Christianity teaches that, by caring for the poor, believers are able to show their love for God. There are many ways in which Christians are encouraged to do this, such as by saving resources, not being greedy for money and possessions, and by donating to charities and organisations that help the poor both in the UK and worldwide. 'The Church should concern itself…with the poor and needy' (Catechism of the Catholic Church).

2 Explain how the teachings of the Bible have enabled one Christian agency to work for the relief of poverty. (8 marks)

Christian Aid is a Christian relief agency set up by the British Council of Churches, working to relieve poverty throughout the world. It provides long-term aid to help the world's poorest communities develop agriculture, education and healthcare. It also gives short-term emergency help to people affected by wars and natural disasters. Christian Aid works with local people and tries to educate the poor to help themselves. It also brings the problems of world poverty to the attention of the leaders and people of the world's richest nations. Christian Aid is involved in many campaigns on behalf of the world's poor.

Its work is founded on the teachings of the Bible. Everybody is equal before God and God has given the riches of the earth for all humans to share, not just the wealthy few. Christian Aid campaigns for wealth and resources to be shared equally among everyone, so that all people can have a decent standard of living: 'If anyone has material possessions and sees his brother in need but has no pity on him, how can the love of God be in him?' (1 John 3:17). At the heart of the work of Christian Aid is the belief that all life is precious to God. Just as Jesus cared for the poor, so Christian Aid seeks to relieve poverty throughout the world. As the Christian Aid *Prayer for a New Earth* states: 'God of all places and this place: you promised a new earth where the hungry will feast and the oppressed go free. Come Lord, build that place among us.'

3 'You cannot be wealthy and be a Christian.' Do you agree? Give reasons for your opinion, showing you have considered another point of view. In your answer, you should refer to at least one religion. (8 marks)

'It is easier for a camel to go through the eye of a needle than for a rich man to enter the kingdom of God' (Mark 10:25).

Since the Bible teaches that it is not wrong to be wealthy, it should be possible to be wealthy and be a Christian. However, it is wrong to be greedy and it must be difficult for people who are obsessed with their wealth to have a relationship with God. This is because wealthy people tend to want more and more money and possessions. In a sense, money becomes their God. As the Bible says: 'You cannot serve both God and Money' (Matthew 6:24).

A Christian should follow the example of Jesus and help the poor because, if it is used properly, wealth can really help those in need. The Bible teaches that Christians should give money to the poor every week. This is called almsgiving. It is possible to be a Christian and be wealthy and religious, but it is hard. Wealthy Christians must understand that their money should be used to help others.

I wonder why we do not seem to hear much in the media about wealthy Christians — Cliff Richard is a well-known example, but it is hard to think of many others. Maybe this is because Christians who are wealthy do not want to admit it. Also, if Christianity teaches that wealth should be shared, why is it that the Christian Church owns so much land and churches are so richly decorated. Could they not sell some of their possessions and help the poor?

I think it is possible to be a wealthy Christian, but it is not easy. The best advice for wealthy Christians is probably to follow the words of Jesus: 'Go, sell everything you have and give it to the poor, and you will have treasure in heaven' (Mark 10:21). However, this could never be practical advice for all Christians, since they would then simply increase the numbers of poor who need financial aid! While this may be the right calling for some rich Christians, finding practical, Godly ways to use their money will probably be more effective for most rich Christians in the long run.

Class activities and homework

Understanding and evaluating Christian teachings concerning wealth

In pairs or small groups, write down three Christian teachings about wealth. Evaluate them by giving reasons why such teachings work, and reasons why they do not work. Under your teacher's guidance, report back to the class. As a class, discuss which teachings are the most and least effective.

How do Christian attitudes towards wealth differ from non-Christian attitudes?

Understanding the causes of poverty in the UK and world-wide

In pairs or small groups, look at a newspaper. Cut out all the stories about poverty in the UK and overseas, and identify what each story suggests is the cause of poverty. Under the guidance of your teacher, make a class list of the causes of poverty. Discuss how far the causes of poverty in the UK are the same as or different from the causes of poverty around the world.

Make two lists: one listing the main causes of poverty in the UK and the other listing causes of poverty in less economically developed countries. Can the problem of poverty ever be solved?

Understanding and evaluating the work of Christian relief agencies

In pairs or small groups, select a Christian relief agency. On a large sheet of paper, write down the ethos of the group and its main areas of work. Look at how this work is carried out. Make a colourful chart or diagram that identifies these ways, including some evaluation of how effective the work is — what is good and what is ineffectual. Discuss as a class how the work of such agencies could be improved.

'It is the responsibility of governments, not relief agencies, to help the poor.' Do you agree? Give reasons for your opinion, showing you have considered another point of view.

Glossary

A

Abortion The termination of the life of a foetus in the womb

Absolute poverty Condition in which people have no money, land or possessions

Active euthanasia Taking active steps to end the life of a patient, for example by giving a lethal injection

Adultery Having a sexual relationship with someone other than your marriage partner

Agnostic Someone who is unsure whether there is sufficient evidence to prove the existence of God

Almsgiving Charitable donations

Appropriate technology Simpe machinery and other tools that help people in the poorest parts of the world to improve their standard of living

Assisted suicide The provision of means and/or opportunity whereby a patient may terminate their life themselves

Atheist Someone who does not believe that God exists or that there is a convincing case for the existence of God

B

Benevolent All-loving

Bigamy Getting married while still married legally to someone else

C

Causation The principle that everything is caused by something else

Charismatic experience An experience inspired by the Holy Spirit, including speaking in tongues and prophecy

Cohabitation A man and woman living together as a married couple without legalising their union through marriage

Communion of saints Christians who have died and gone to heaven, and who continue to be part of the Christian community on earth

Contraception A range of methods that may be used to prevent conception

Conversion experience Transferring faith from one religion to another, or from non-belief to belief in God

D

Design The principle that things with a purpose and function have been designed for that purpose

Development Changes that improve people's lives

Divorce The legal termination of a marriage

Dualism The view that there are two natures or sides to everything: a physical (seen) side and a spiritual (unseen) side

E

Empirical evidence Evidence confirmed using the senses

Equality Treating people in the same way irrespective of sex, race, education, disability or any other factor that may set them apart

Eternal The belief that God exists without beginning and end

Euthanasia Literally a 'good' or 'happy' death; usually refers to mercy killing or prematurely ending the life of a terminally ill patient

Exclusivism The view that only those who belong to one particular faith can be saved from condemnation

Extended family Parents, children and perhaps other relations such as grandparents, aunts, uncles and cousins all living together or close enough to see each other regularly

F

Faith Belief in something (e.g. God) without proof

Faithfulness Maintaining a sexual relationship with the same person

G

Heaven A place where, after death, humans can live eternally in the presence of God; other interpretations suggest that heaven is an *idea* in the minds of believers rather than an actual place

Hell Traditionally, a place where unrepentant souls are eternally punished after death; modern interpretations may refer to hell as the absence of God or even suggest that the evils of hell are experienced on earth rather than after death

Heterosexuality Sexual attraction to members of the opposite sex

Homosexuality Sexual attraction to members of the same sex

H

Immortal soul A soul which can live on after the death of the physical body

Immutable The belief that God's nature and characteristics do not change

Inclusivism The view that all religions have some truth and should be able to teach and practise without restriction or prejudice

Inconsistent triad The logical problem of how evil can exist alongside an omnipotent, all-loving God

Involuntary euthanasia Ending the life of a patient who is not able to make the request for themselves

LEDCs Less economically developed countries

M

Marriage The legal union of a man and a woman

Miracle An event that violates natural law and has a beneficial outcome

Monogamy Being married to only one person

Moral evil Evil acts performed by humans

Moral responsibility An obligation to help other people which the law cannot enforce

Multi-ethnic A society that consists of people from different cultural backgrounds

Multi-faith A society that consists of people from different faiths

Multi-racial A society that consists of people from different racial backgrounds

Mystical experience Hearing God's voice or seeing a vision of a religious figure

National poverty line A measurement used by the UK government; those living below a certain level of income are said to live below the poverty line

Natural evil Events in the natural world that cause suffering

Near-death experience An experience after clinical death when a patient may see bright lights, a religious figure and sense being sent back to earth

Nuclear family Two parents and their children all living together

Numinous experience An experience that conveys a sense of awe and wonder

Omnipotent All-powerful

Omniscient All-knowing

P

Paranormal Experiences that suggest there may be a non-visible, spirit world, for example ghosts or communications through mediums

Passive euthanasia Withdrawing medical treatment or nourishment to hasten the death of a patient

Polygamy Being married to more than one person at the same time

Possessions Material things which people possess or own

Poverty Lack of money, land and possessions

Prayer Communicating with God through words or meditation, alone or with others

Pre-marital sex Sexual intercourse prior to marriage

Promiscuity A lifestyle characterised by casual sexual relationships

Purgatory The place where souls go after death to be purified for heaven

Racial discrimination Treating people less favourably, and considering them to be less worthy, on the grounds of their race

Racial harmony A society in which people of different races live together in peace

Racial prejudice The view that certain races are inferior or superior

Reconstituted family Where a man and woman, who have children by previous relationships, are married and the two families become one

Rehabilitation Equipping people, such as drug addicts, with the things they need to return to everyday life

Relative poverty Poverty in a society where most people have some money, land or possessions

Religious experience An experience that conveys a sense of the presence of God

Religious freedom Members of all religions are free to worship and have equal political rights

Religious pluralism An acceptance of all faiths as having equal rights to co-exist

Resurrection The view that, after death, God recreates a new body in a heavenly place

S

Sanctity of life The principle that life is sacred (holy) because God created it

Secular A non-religious view, society or organisation

Sexism Judging a person less favourably on the grounds of their sex

Single-parent family One parent living alone with their children; this may be due to divorce, separation, the death of the other partner or because the parent is unmarried

Stewardship Taking care of something that does not belong to you

T

Theist Someone who believes in the traditional idea of God, usually as omnipotent, omniscient and benevolent

Tithe The Christian idea of committing 10% of income to the Church or another religious organisation

Tokenism Including one or two members of racial minorities to ensure that no claim can be made of racism

V

Verified Proved to be true

Voluntary euthanasia Ending the life of a patient at their request

W

Wealth Money, land and possessions

World development The need for rich and poor nations to work together to relieve world poverty

Z

Zakah Committing 2.5% of income and savings for the relief of suffering in the Muslim community

Useful websites

Islam

These websites provide answers to questions about Islam, Islamic–Christian relations, and Islamic responses to world and social issues:

www.answering-islam.org.uk   www.islam101.com   www.islamonline.net

Religious, ethical and cultural issues in the media

The BBC website features regularly changing articles on religious and ethical issues in the news: www.bbc.co.uk/religion

Channel 4's webpage on religious and cultural issues is usually linked to relevant programmes on its network: www.channel4.com/culture

Faithhealers

This website exposes faith healers such as Benny Hinn:

www.fakefaithhealers.com

Christian marriage

www.christianmarriage.com

Science and religion

www.answersingenesis.org

Charities

www.cafod.org.uk   www.care.org.uk   www.christian-aid.org.uk
www.leonard-cheshire.org   www.muslimaid.org   www.salvationarmy.org.uk

Revision

The BBC GCSE Bitesize website is focused on revision. It contains summaries of key topics and practice tests:

www.bbc.co.uk/schools/gcsebitesize/re

These websites contain articles on Christian philosophy and ethics which are useful for revision:

www.beliefnet.com   www.christiantopics.com   www.faithnet.org

Index

A

abortion(s)   *35–40, 44–45, 47*
absolute poverty   *125*
active euthanasia   *40*
adultery   *49–52, 59, 67–68*
advance directives
  (living wills)   *40–41, 43–44*
afterlife   *5, 27–35, 126*
agnostic(s)   *14, 24*
Al-Sunnah   *4*
almsgiving   *123*
annulment   *60–61*
assisted suicide   *41, 44*
atheist(s)   *14, 16, 21, 24*

B

baptism   *3, 63*
benevolence of God   *18*
bigamy   *54*
Big Bang   *16*
Bonnke, Reinhardt   *102–103*
Booth, William   *129*
Bush, George W.   *102, 103, 104*

C

cash crops   *131*
causation   *12*
charismatic experience   *6*
charities
  CAFOD   *134–135*
  Christian Aid   *132–134, 137*
  Christian Alliance Housing
    Association   *128*
  Church Urban Fund   *128*
  Leonard Cheshire Foundation   *128–129*
  Muslim Aid   *136*
  Salvation Army   *129*
  Shaftesbury Society   *128*
Cheshire, Leonard   *128–129*
cohabitation   *53, 67*

communion of saints   *30*
compatibilism   *16*
contraception   *38, 52–53*
Cosmological Argument   *12*

D

Darwin, Charles   *15*
Dawkins, Richard   *15, 104*
Day of Judgement   *30–31*
debt   *128, 131*
design   *12*
developed countries   *130*
developing countries   *130*
divorce   *50, 53, 54, 59–62, 67, 70*
documentaries
  Everyman   *117*
  God Bless America   *103*
  Running for God   *103, 114*
  Some of my Best Friends are…   *114*
  Teenage Texan Virgins   *100*
  The Big Question: Why Are We Here?   *104*
  Turning Muslim in Texas   *101*
double effect   *42*

E

empirical evidence   *1*
equality   *56, 73–74*
euthanasia   *40–44, 46–47*
evil and suffering   *17–19*
exclusivism   *81*
extended family   *62*

F

faith   *1*
family   *62, 64, 68–69*
films
  Gattaca   *105*
  Priest   *108*
  Yentl   *110*
free will   *18–19*